To Madeleine
With best wishes
Gaye Mitchell

WORLD ON FIRE

SAVING AN ENDANGERED EARTH

Senator George J. Mitchell

Charles Scribner's Sons
New York
Collier Macmillan Canada
Toronto
Maxwell Macmillan International
New York   Oxford   Singapore   Sydney

Charles Scribner's Sons
Macmillan Publishing Company
866 Third Avenue, New York, NY 10022

Collier Macmillan Canada, Inc.
1200 Eglinton Avenue East, Suite 200
Don Mills, Ontario M3C 3N1

Library of Congress Cataloging-in-Publication Data

Mitchell, George J. (George John), 1933–
    World on fire : saving an endangered earth / by George J.
Mitchell.
        p.   cm.
    Includes bibliographical references and index.
    ISBN 0-684-19231-4
    1. Greenhouse effect, Atmospheric.   2. Environmental protection.
I. Title.
QC912.3.M57   1991
363.73'87—dc20   90-8578
                                                                             CIP

Macmillan books are available at special discounts for bulk purchases for
sales promotions, premiums, fund-raising, or educational use.
For details, contact:

Special Sales Director
Macmillan Publishing Company
866 Third Avenue
New York, NY 10022

10 9 8 7 6 5 4 3 2 1

Designed by Nancy Sugihara

Printed in the United States of America

Contents

PART 2

SAVING THE PLANET

Acknowledgments

Many people contributed to the creation of this book. I am grateful to all of them. Six deserve special mention.

Mike Hamilburg suggested the book and guided me through its writing and publication. He is not so much an agent as he is a friend, close and valued. He also did me the enormous favor of introducing me to Jack Waugh.

Jack is a brilliant writer, researcher, and editor. Without his assistance, the writing of this book would not have been possible.

With his prodding and cajoling, Ned Chase stimulated my thinking and writing. He is a writer's editor.

Dr. Michael Oppenheimer and Nicholas Lenssen reviewed the manuscript, detected and corrected errors, and made many valuable suggestions for improvement. Any errors that may remain are, of course, mine.

The person who most influenced the writing of this book does not yet know of its existence. Edmund S. Muskie served the people of Maine and the nation as governor, senator, and secretary of state. He is, in my opinion, the greatest public figure in Maine's history. He also is, by universal acclaim, the greatest environmental legislator in American history. Almost single-

handedly, he created the Clean Water Act, the Clean Air Act, and most of the other laws that have done so much to protect the American people and their natural environment.

To me, Ed Muskie is predecessor, mentor, hero. I first became involved in public service because of him. From him I first gained meaningful knowledge of the threat to our environment and the need to protect it. His integrity and intellect, his high concept of public service, have served as guides and goals for me. This book is dedicated to him.

Portland, Maine
May 1990

PART 1

INTO THE GREENHOUSE CENTURY

The future is no longer what it used to be.

PAUL VALÉRY

1

The Politics of the Environment

It was 10:30 in the morning when the meeting broke up. We were tired and discouraged. A sense of failure engulfed the room and troubled everyone in it.

For more than three weeks we had been meeting in my office in the Capitol, just a few feet from the Senate chamber. We had worked our way, slowly and with great difficulty, through several tough issues, such as controls on toxic and other air pollutants emitted from stationary sources. But we had reached an impasse on the vexing question of how much to reduce motor vehicle emissions, and by when. After three long days of haggling, of proposals and counterproposals, of charges and countercharges, culminating in this almost all-night session, we broke up in disagreement.

As I left for home, I thought the effort was over and the clean air bill doomed. We couldn't reach agreement. So we'd have to fight it out on the Senate floor. There, I knew, the prospects for passing the bill were not good.

President Bush was adamantly opposed to the tougher controls on motor vehicle emissions that I and most of the other members of the Senate Environment Committee thought were necessary.

3

Mr. Bush had proclaimed himself the Environmental President; his speeches were filled with the rhetoric of the green movement. But when it came to real action, to specific legislation, the Bush administration's deeds did not match the president's words.

In my office, as we hammered out the clean air bill—word by word, line by line—there was no environmental rhetoric from the president's men. Their concern was the cost to industry— the auto industry, the oil industry, steel, chemical, coal, utilities. We can't do this; it will cost too much. We can't do that; industry can't afford it. Over and over they urged less control, stressed cost, argued for delay. I sometimes wondered if they had read the Environmental President's speeches!

I was frustrated, even angry, because I knew that we couldn't pass the bill over the president's opposition. Even if every one of the fifty-five Democrats in the Senate supported the bill, there were enough Republicans to block action. And I knew very well that I couldn't get the support of every Democrat. Several of them would join the president in killing the bill. The clean air bill was likely to fail again, as it had for the past thirteen years.

For nearly a decade I had struggled to pass a clean air bill. Twice before, the Senate Environment Committee had approved my legislation to control acid rain. Both times I couldn't get the bill to the full Senate for consideration, and it died. Now I am the majority leader in the Senate. I decide which bills will or will not come before the full Senate for consideration. As I had often said I would, I used my authority to bring the clean air bill before the Senate. And so, finally, the debate began.

As I had anticipated, it quickly became evident that there weren't enough votes to pass the bill as reported by the committee. The president opposed it. That took away the support of most Republican senators. There were enough Democrats who would join them to form a majority against the bill.

I realized that there was a difference between the best and strongest bill in the abstract and the best and strongest bill that could pass the Senate. The committee bill was the former. Now

we had to find the latter. To do that I convened and presided over negotiations with the president's staff. It was something I had seen coming.

In 1977, under the leadership of my predecessor, Senator Edmund S. Muskie of Maine, Congress amended the Clean Air Act to require all areas of the country to come into compliance with federal air quality standards. The 1977 amendments were hailed as a significant advance in environmental protection. The five-year target was considered reasonable, the objective of clean air nationally deemed attainable.

But it didn't happen. The air wasn't clean by 1982. The law was changed and the target was postponed to 1987, then postponed again, and yet again. More and more American cities found their air deteriorating, until by 1989 nearly half of all Americans breathed air that did not meet the health-based standards of federal law.

Through the 1980s the number of Americans grew steadily, as did the number of their motor vehicles and the total miles those vehicles were driven. The number of stationary sources of air pollution also grew—electric utility generating plants, factories, industrial complexes—as did their emissions. And, most worrisome, the number of Americans who fell ill and died from exposure to air pollution also rose.

Despite the grim statistics, the law remained for thirteen years inadequate and unchanged. This happened for many reasons: the hostility of President Reagan to all environmental legislation; the concern of many members of Congress about the effect of tough antipollution laws on the economies of their states; the scope and complexity of the problem; the huge cost of dealing with it; and the scientific uncertainty that remained about the precise causes and effects of air pollution.

In 1981, a year after entering the Senate, I introduced the first bill to control acid rain. For nine years, I struggled to call attention to what I believed to be a serious and growing national problem. Gradually, the public's awareness grew. Study after

study produced new data about acid rain and toxic air pollution. The ghastly accident at Bhopal, India, the discovery of the hole in the ozone layer, the large-scale deforestation in Brazil—all these made headlines and fueled public demand for action.

At last, on January 23, 1990, after thirteen years of inaction, the Senate began consideration of comprehensive clean air legislation. It took just a few seconds to formally start the process. Addressing the presiding officer, I said:

> Mr. President: Following the conclusion of morning business at 3:30 P.M., I will seek unanimous consent to proceed to the consideration of Calendar Item No. 427, that is S.1630, the Clean Air legislation.

Behind those few words lay a year of struggle to draft and shape the legislation. The first and most important breakthrough was the departure of Ronald Reagan from the presidency. Never in modern American history has a president been so hostile to the notion of environmental protection. From his famous assertion that trees cause pollution (an assertion that prompted a student at the University of California to hang a sign on a tree that read: Chop me down before I kill again!) to less well-known incidents of obstruction, the eight years of the Reagan presidency were a low point for the American environment.

Not only did his administration slash funding for environmental protection, it also tried to repeal or weaken the environmental laws already in place. And when it largely failed to do that, it simply refused to enforce the law. Officials charged with upholding the law deliberately obstructed its enforcement instead. Chaos and despair descended on the Environmental Protection Agency. One high-level official went to jail, others resigned under fire. Members of Congress concerned about the environment—Democrats and Republicans—fought a rearguard action to prevent the cuts from being too deep, to stop the efforts to repeal or weaken, to take modest new initiatives where possible. It was a dark and difficult time.

The election of 1988 promised change. Both George Bush and Michael Dukakis proclaimed themselves environmentalists and promised to propose and support clean air legislation. Following his election, Bush made good on that promise. In the summer of 1989, he sent a clean air proposal to Congress. Although disappointing in some respects, and somewhat pallid in contrast to his soaring rhetoric on the subject, the president's proposal, merely by virtue of his having made it, decisively shifted the balance on the issue. With the president for action instead of adamantly against it, the focus turned to what kind of bill to pass, not whether any bill should be passed at all.

As the Senate Committee on Environment and Public Works struggled through day after day of hearings on the subject and moved toward the actual writing of the bill, I became concerned about the attitude that was developing in the administration. In public, the president made sweeping, general statements obviously intended to enhance his claim to be an environmentalist. But in private, the heavy emphasis of the president's aides was on cost, on what could not be done rather than on what should be done.

I felt that the president's bill, while a very positive step, was not broad enough or strong enough to deal effectively with the problem. I also knew that the subject was so controversial—and therefore unpopular with members of Congress—that whatever happened in this Congress, it would likely be a long time before we revisited the subject. We had to do it now, and we had to do it right—or at least as nearly right as was politically possible.

I anticipated a long, controversial debate in the Senate on the bill and I searched for a way to gain some leverage in what, it was becoming increasingly clear, would be a struggle to pass anything stronger than the president's bill. As the committee began to write the bill, the question answered itself.

Most of the committee's members had joined it because of their concern for the environment. Even those who joined it for other reasons had a hard time not sharing that concern once they

were exposed to the growing evidence of the seriousness of the problem. In addition, the membership of the committee was not geographically representative of the nation; there were no members from the Midwest, while New England and the West were overrepresented. Environmental concern ran high on the committee.

As the bill took shape, it became obvious that it would be much stronger than the president's bill. Indeed, I thought, it might be like some of the committee's previous efforts, too strong to pass the Senate. But, in this instance, it would be useful to have a strong committee bill to use as a standard against which to measure the president's bill—and toward which to move the president's bill. I soon learned that my strategy was right; I later learned it was also wrong.

The struggle was far from over with Senate consideration of the bill. In some important respects, it had just begun.

The distinguishing feature of the United States Senate is the right of unlimited debate. A senator may speak for as long as he or she wishes on any subject at any time. Invoking this right, a group of senators, although only a minority of the full Senate, may delay or prevent the body from acting on any given issue. To overcome this tactic, a "super majority" of sixty senators must vote to terminate debate.

Soon after I brought the clean air bill to the floor for debate in January, it became clear to me that there were not sixty senators willing to terminate debate and pass the bill. It was just too controversial. The auto industry, the oil industry, the steel industry, the coal industry, the electric utility industry, the petrochemical industry—and a host of others—organized to defeat the bill. They were for clean air—they said—but they couldn't afford to do what was necessary to achieve it; or, at least, what the bill demanded they do to achieve it.

So they organized, under the misnomer "The Clean Air Working Group." In fact the only thing this group worked for was to prevent the passage of clean air legislation. But they spent a

lot of money. They objected and they obstructed, and—unfortunately—they found a receptive ally in the Bush administration. The committee had reported its bill in November. That bill, S.1630, dealt with five subjects: acid rain, toxic air pollutants, chlorofluorocarbons (CFCs), emissions from stationary sources, and emissions from mobile sources (motor vehicles). It incorporated about 80 percent of what the president had earlier recommended. But it went beyond the president's recommendations in several important respects, particularly toxic air pollutants, CFCs, and mobile source emissions.

Responding to industrial concerns, the administration refused to embrace the committee bill, even though it largely incorporated the president's recommendations. Instead, the administration devoted all of its considerable influence and energy to opposing the bill because of the provisions in it with which the administration disagreed.

Unable to muster the sixty votes necessary to terminate the filibuster, largely because of the president's opposition, I had a choice: I could insist on a vote to end the filibuster; a loss would throw the issue into confusion, a bad loss could result in no bill being passed at all. Or I could negotiate with the administration, and with individual senators who had specific objections to the bill, and try to win over enough converts to get the necessary sixty votes. I chose to negotiate. The risk of not doing so was too high.

We began in my office on February 2, 1990, as the full Senate turned temporarily to other matters. The low point came in late February, on that morning after three days of haggling, when we reached an impasse on the question of mobile source emissions. But by the next day, both sides were ready to resume the negotiations and, after another day of hard bargaining, we broke the impasse. The compromise enabled the administration to assert that only one round of reductions of mobile source emissions will be required, that to occur in this decade. But in fact, given the history of the Clean Air Act and the continuing increase in

motor vehicle miles driven, it is virtually certain that a second round of such resolutions will be required in the first decade of the next century.

Finally, after nearly one month, two dozen meetings, and over 250 hours of negotiation, we had reached agreement. In the process, I learned why my strategy had been right. The negotiations involved over fifty senators, hundreds of staffers, and dozens of administration officials. But it was essentially between the Senate Committee on the Environment with its bill and the Bush administration with its bill. The committee bill served precisely the purpose I had envisioned for it: a lever to force the administration to move beyond its bill. The compromise was not as broad or as strong as the committee bill, but it was much broader and stronger than the president's bill. I announced the agreement on March 1, and learned immediately why my strategy had been wrong.

Something had happened which I had not anticipated: The committee bill had become the minimum acceptable bill to most of the national environmental organizations and much of the press. Rather than praising the committee for getting the president to move beyond his bill, they criticized us for accepting anything less than our bill. Most importantly, in the debate over the differences between the president's bill and the committee bill, the dramatic improvements which the compromise made over current law were obscured.

On March 2, the *New York Times* headlined the agreement as a "dilution" of the committee bill. The accompanying story was devoted largely to a description of the differences between the "stronger" committee bill and the "weaker" compromise bill. That perception made more difficult the task of getting the compromise bill passed by the Senate.

That process was already complicated. The Senate routinely disposes of bills in a couple of legislative days, sometimes less. Controversial bills may take a week or two. Rarely does a bill consume a month of active consideration on the Senate floor. That is how long the clean air bill took.

On April 3, more than two months after the Senate first took up the measure, the Senate finally passed the clean air bill. At last we had committed ourselves to strong action to clean up America's polluted air. It was a vote I had worked for and waited to see for a decade.

As I write these words in early May, 1990, in the aftermath of the Senate vote, I am gratified by the progress so far, difficult as it was. But I recognize that there is still a long, hard legislative road to travel before this bill becomes law. The House of Representatives has yet to act. If and when it does, its bill will certainly differ in some respects—perhaps many—from the Senate version. That will make a conference between the two houses necessary to reconcile the differences. The product of that conference will then have to be passed again by both bodies before it goes to the president for his signature.

Although what the president finally signs into law will no doubt differ from the bill passed by the Senate, that bill was important because it established the agenda for action. It was a significant expansion of and improvement upon current law. Among its provisions that break new ground are:

- A complete phaseout of CFCs by the year 2000.
- Substantial reductions in sulfur dioxide and nitrogen oxides, the precursors of acid rain.
- Tighter controls on emissions of toxic air pollutants. Under current law, seven such pollutants have been regulated in the past twenty years. The new bill requires 187 more to be regulated within two years; industries must install the maximum achievable technology to control them within three years thereafter.
- Reductions in emissions from the tail pipes of automobiles and light trucks, the first such new limits in thirteen years. The first phase of these reductions will occur in this decade; a second phase will lock in for all such vehicles, if necessary, beginning in the model year 2004.
- In those areas of the country in which the air does not meet

the law's standard, specific measures will be required to achieve annual reductions of emissions of at least 3 percent until the standard is met.

These and the other provisions of the legislation (the bill is nearly six hundred pages long and highly technical, so I list here only a very brief summary of its most important parts) will, if enacted, surely improve the quality of the air Americans breathe.

But beyond any doubt, further, more drastic action will have to be taken. As difficult as it may be to pass the clean air bill, we must recognize that it is but a modest first step.

In this book I attempt to describe not only the problem of clean air, but also the global threat to our environment across the board. I attempt to suggest what must be done, and why. Just as the human race has met and surmounted every previous challenge to its survival, so, I am confident, will it meet and surmount this one. But that will require knowledge, the commitment of large resources, and a supreme effort on the part of the governments and peoples of all nations. Most of all, it will require changes in the way we live.

2

Two Children in a Future World

Journey with me for a moment into the twenty-first century and meet two children, Luisa and Eric. Luisa lives in Mexico City sometime in the next century, about fifty years from now. She looks up at a polluted sky in this future world and sees no sun at all. In all her young life—she is now nine—she has rarely seen the sun.

She has heard that Mexico City was once a beautiful place to live. There was plenty of sun once and a lot more room.

There was plenty of sun on the cool, clear November day in the year 1519, some six centuries before Luisa was born, when the Spaniard Diego de Ordaz stood in a high mountain pass and looked down on the Valley of Mexico for the first time. It was one of the most spectacular sights on earth and he was the first European to see it.

The valley was an elevated plain a mile and a half above sea level, surrounded by rugged snow-capped mountain ranges and covering an area of nearly a thousand square miles. Near its center lay five large interconnected lakes. On a small island in one of those lakes sat the city of Tenochtitlán, then the seat of the Aztec Empire, and the future center of Mexico City.

Ordaz and his coterie of Spanish soldiers and their commander, Hernán Cortés, were near the end of a three-month march from Vera Cruz to the Aztec capital. In a short time they would complete the conquest of the Aztecs and change forever the history of Central and South America. They also would set in motion events that would transform the magnificent valley they now entered.

In Ordaz's day the Valley of Mexico was a place of great natural beauty. Even in Luisa's century it remains a spectacular setting. But it was also a setting for a man-made disaster, of a type and magnitude that neither the Aztecs nor their Spanish conquerors could have foreseen.

Much has happened in the valley since the sixteenth century. By the 1990s, fifty years before Luisa was born, nearly twenty million people lived in the metropolitan Mexico City area, working at thirty-six thousand industrial facilities and driving over three million motor vehicles, which they kept an average of twelve years. Mexico hadn't required any emission control devices on motor vehicles until 1992. The combustion of gasoline is only two-thirds as efficient at Mexico City's mile-and-a-half elevation as it is at sea level. The combination of no control devices and the high elevation began devastating Mexico City's air.

Toward the end of the twentieth century five and a half million tons of contaminants were being emitted into the atmosphere above the city each year. Regularly, and especially in the cool winter months, warm air passing over the surrounding mountains trapped the cooler air in the valley. There, stagnant and close to the ground, the pollution sickened people and sometimes killed them.

Lead, hydrocarbons, nitrogen oxides, and sulfur dioxide poisoned the air. All were unhealthy, but lead was the most dangerous. It killed some people. It slowed mental development in others. Although the level of lead in Mexican gasoline was gradually reduced, it continued to remain dangerously high.

Many people began experiencing dizziness, drowsiness, shortness of breath, irritation of the eyes and lungs, and a wide range

of respiratory ailments. And it was hardest of all on the narrow airways of young children.

Bad as it was before the turn of the century, Mexico City's air only got worse in the years before Luisa was born. The government's efforts to control air pollution—improved gasoline, reduced use of motor vehicles, some emission controls—were simply overwhelmed by growth. The population of Mexico had begun exploding in the twentieth century, and as it continued to grow the air over its capital city became more and more polluted. In 1910 there had been about 15 million Mexicans. By 1950 there were 25 million. By 1990 there were more than 85 million. Very soon there were 100 million, then 150 million. Much of that growth was centered in Mexico City.

By the year 2000—the dawn of Luisa's century—there were more than thirty million people driving nine million motor vehicles in the Valley of Mexico. The valley of the Aztecs, that high plateau of such surpassing beauty, had become a valley of death.

It was not alone. By then the metropolitan areas of Tokyo and São Paulo also had populations of more than thirty million; New York, Seoul, and Bombay had reached twenty million. Inexorably the number of motor vehicles on the streets of these cities increased with the population, and so did the pollution.

In the decade before the year 2000 there were five billion people in the world. Sometime in Luisa's century, the ten-billionth person would be born. Most of this jump in population had taken place in the less-developed countries. And so had the biggest increase in the number and use of motor vehicles. There were about five hundred million registered motor vehicles on earth late in the twentieth century. Their numbers continued increasing twice as fast as the numbers of people. When the population of the world reaches ten billion the number of motor vehicles will hit two billion.

Now, near the middle of Luisa's century, a dark, gray-brown shroud hanging low over Mexico City is a fact of daily life. It makes each breath an irritating effort and it shuts out the sun.

Luisa's world is not only without sun but without hope. There

are now too many people crammed into her city, living too close together. It is doubtful in this teeming environment that she will live to be thirty-five. Two of her brothers and many of her friends have already died. It doesn't seem fair to her that people should be dying so young and that the sky should be so dark.

But this is the twenty-first century, and that's the way the world is.

Half a continent away in this world of the twenty-first century, in the United States in a place called North Dakota, a boy of Luisa's age named Eric has a quite different kind of problem with the sun.

The summer will come and Eric, too, will see little of it. He will have to stay indoors again, where he has spent all of his nine summers.

It isn't at all like it was when his grandfather was growing up, when boys lived out in the sun all summer long, from the minute school let out in June until it started again in September.

Even Eric's father and mother had been able to play outside on summer days, down by the creek or along the railroad tracks, when they were growing up. And they hadn't had to wear protective clothing. Pictures in old magazines showed kids in the twentieth century out under the sun with no shirts on at all. They thought nothing of going out in the middle of the day. They didn't even care what they wore and often as not wore hardly anything. In Eric's world that would be unthinkable.

To him life in North Dakota doesn't seem any more fair than it does to Luisa in Mexico City. Unlike her, he has about everything else he could wish for. His parents don't lack for money. He has his own room and plenty of things to play with. His parents have been very successful. But even they don't go outdoors in the summer anymore without their protective clothing and sunglasses.

And it is all because of a hole in the sky.

The scientists had detected the hole more than fifty years ago, late in the twentieth century. It had appeared first in the ozone

layer of the stratosphere over the Antarctic, and it was bigger than the continent itself. Then a big ozone loss was discovered in the Northern Hemisphere centered on a hole over the North Pole. Now rifts in the ozone layer have spread over the more-inhabited parts of the globe.

As every kid in North Dakota now knows, when there is no ozone layer in the stratosphere there is nothing to keep out the sun's ultraviolet radiation. Its rays, unfiltered by the ozone, beam down to earth and cause skin cancer. It wasn't long after the turn of the century that people began getting cancer and dying in epidemic numbers. Since then, kids like Eric just don't spend their summers under the sun.

But this is the twenty-first century, and that's the way the world is.

Is such a future world possible? Yes.
Can it be averted? Yes.
Will it be averted? That depends on us.

3

What Is Happening

This future world in which Eric and Luisa live is not an Orwellian fantasy or a page from Aldous Huxley. It is a world already in the making. We ourselves have set the planet on that course. If we do not do something to change it, it will be our world within a century.

Such a prospect saddens and alarms me. I was born and raised in Maine. I saw there the best and the worst of the relationship between human beings and their environment. Maine is a state of great natural beauty. Few places on earth can match the coast of "Down East" Maine, where mountain, forest, and ocean meet. Few places can compare with unsettled northern Maine, where no man-made structures intrude on hundreds of miles of rolling hills covered with forests and studded with lakes.

But the Maine of my boyhood was also the place of ill-regulated industrial emissions and municipal wastes that together were turning the state's major rivers into open sewers. My first years were spent in a home directly overlooking the Kennebec River. It was then filthy and foul-smelling, filled with waste and covered with scum. The riverfront then was a slum. Now property on the water's edge is in demand, because the Kennebec and other Maine rivers are once again clean.

19

They are clean because my predecessor in the Senate, Edmund S. Muskie, led the fight to pass the first federal Clean Water Act. One of the most successful federal programs in our history, that act reversed decades of decline in the quality of the nation's waters. Now we must do the same with our air. And we must do the same with a threatened global environment.

My Maine upbringing kindled in me a lifelong commitment to our environmental well-being. I see that well-being in peril today, the greatest peril it has ever faced. I fear that unless we do something to stem the destructive environmental forces now afoot on our planet, no children in the future, not just a mythical Luisa and a mythical Eric, will ever experience a pollution-free life. And that will be a tragedy.

Planet Earth is sending out distress signals. They carry ominous messages. They tell us that the world is about to grow warmer, warmer than at any time in recorded history, and that the warmth will bring catastrophe. They tell us that holes as wide as the United States and as deep as Mount Everest are being ripped in our stratosphere's ozone layer, which is our only protection from the lethal ultraviolet rays of the sun. They tell us that the planet's vast tropical rain forests, so rich in life and so necessary to it, are being stripped away at a breakneck pace—nearly an acre every second—turning once-lush, teeming portions of earth into farm-land, bushland, grassland, or desert. And they tell us that a silent stalker, acid rain, continues to fall like a shroud over our planet, killing plant life on land and fish in the water and threatening human health.

These four dark phenomena—all of them the creations of humankind—are a figurative Four Horsemen of the Apocalypse riding over today's world environment. And when they have passed by, what will be left is the nightmare world of Luisa and Eric.

The greenhouse effect is not a theory. It is not a mathematical model. It is a reality. America's three leading scientific academies have warned us that humans are daily plying earth's systems with

new stresses that could trigger traumatic climatic surprises and devastation worldwide in the years and decades ahead. Mostafa Kamal Tolba, the executive director of the environmental arm of the United Nations, is even more blunt. He calls what is happening an "ecological holocaust." "Our planet—and countless mysteries of biological life within it," he says, "remains under siege."

Some scientists are now telling us that the warming may not be as bad as we feared. We have heard recently that acid rain, a menace I have struggled to legislate against for a decade in the U.S. Senate, may not be as much of a disaster as we once thought. I hope they are right. But we cannot count on it. I cannot base my decisions as a legislator and a policymaker on those reassuring assumptions. Everything I have seen and read, all the testimony I have heard in Senate hearing rooms, tells me that we cannot afford to take a chance. We must continue to assume that the planet remains under siege and act accordingly.

This ecological holocaust Tolba speaks of has not developed overnight. It has been building for a century. And until recently we have been paying scant attention. The Four Horsemen ride slowly and silently. A "grim specter," as Rachel Carson said of life-threatening pesticides two decades ago in her book *Silent Spring*, "has crept upon us almost unnoticed." The specter has come again in a form even more appalling.

If we cannot check this deadly quartet now loose on our planet and in our atmosphere, life as we know it will change dramatically in the twenty-first century, and much of it will end. This terrible foursome—the greenhouse warming of the planet, the rifts in the ozone layer of the stratosphere, life-killing acid rain in the skies, and wholesale tropical deforestation on the ground—are bringing global environmental catastrophe. They are killing our water, our air, our plants, our animals, and eventually, if not checked, they will kill us. Together they present us with the most pervading international security problem of the coming century, a lethal and long-term threat, the most serious pollution challenge in human history.

We have long suspected this. But in the summer of 1988 something happened to confirm our worst suspicions.

The Summer of 1988

As the spring began to change into summer in the United States in 1988, it seemed to be warmer and dryer than usual. And when summer came, it seemed hot—uncommonly hot. I remember it very well; August in Washington, never benign, seemed more oppressive than normal. Severe drought began setting in with the sweltering heat, searing the North American breadbasket and cutting deeply into the summer grain harvests. Water levels in the lakes fell; the prairie potholes dried up, driving out thousands of ducks that had called them home. The Mississippi River dropped to its lowest level since records have been kept, halting traffic on the river. An inordinate number of forest fires flared through the American West. Four of every ten counties in the United States were put on a drought disaster list.

Drought always brings its own special kind of chaos, much of it plainly evident in the parched land. Taken to its extremes, drought can bring starvation to millions, as it has done repeatedly in Africa in the past and continues to do in the present; or it can turn a fertile prairie into a dust bowl, as it did in Oklahoma in the 1930s. But it can also trigger disastrous chains of events that go unseen, unsuspected, and unfelt until the damage is done. Consider what drought, coming at a critical and inopportune time, can do to a cornfield. The dryness that is drought brings excessive evaporation. And this in turn throws off the timing of pollination, which in corn has a narrow ten-day window. When the window is missed or nearly missed it can mean undeveloped ears of corn, or no ears at all. As a rule of thumb, yields of corn in the U.S. fall by 10 percent for each day the crop is under severe stress during its delicate silking and tasseling stage. Five days of inordinate drought or comparable stress during the critical ten-day window could cut the yield in half. Three midwestern corn harvests since 1950 have been thrown out of their rhythm

in this fashion—all of them in the 1980s. The corn yield per acre dropped 17 percent in the drought of 1980, and 28 percent in the drought of 1983. The summer of 1988 was the worst of all. The corn harvest fell by 34 percent.

The summer of 1988 was, in short, a historic event for the environment. There were record levels of heat, record high levels of ground-level ozone, record drought, and record levels of forest fires. North America was among the hardest hit of all the continents. The summer wasn't as hot and dry everywhere in the world as it was in the U.S., but it was hot enough, the hottest year on record worldwide. Unprecedented heat waves swept simultaneously over the USSR, Asia, and North Africa. A devastating drought prostrated China; soaring temperatures in the Yangtze Valley overwhelmed local hospitals with heatstroke victims. The extraordinary drought that had been parching Africa's Sahel for much of the 1980s continued without letup. And the blazing summer and its drought brought the steepest one-year drop in world grain stock ever recorded. For the first time in long memory the unthinkable happened: A U.S. grain harvest fell below the consumption level, sending waves of apprehension and concern through the world's agricultural economies. Many more such summers and the U.S. would be face-to-face with a prospect even more unthinkable—a loss of food security. It would be a loss felt around the world.

The heat and the drought were not the only disasters of 1988. Hurricane Gilbert rose up out of the Caribbean that summer, slamming into Jamaica, pounding Mexico, and becoming the most severe hurricane ever recorded in the Western Hemisphere. In the late summer, a massive deluge inundated 80 percent of Bangladesh's low-lying land mass, killing more than 1,200 people and displacing 25 million others. Only weeks earlier and a continent away, Khartoum was inundated by the worst flood to hit the Sudan in this century. The city's communications and transportation systems were wiped out and 1.5 million Sudanese became environmental refugees.

There was an eerie sameness to those two summertime floods.

In both cases they had been preceded by several decades of burgeoning population growth around the headwaters of two great river systems, the Ganges and the Nile. Because people must survive however they can, these booming populations at both of the great headwaters stripped away the forests, overgrazed the land, and turned to unstable farming practices. Within forty years half to three-fourths of the middle mountain range in Nepal on the Ganges above Bangladesh had been laid bare. Thus stripped, the Himalayas could no longer hold back the powerful monsoon. And the deltas downriver in Bangladesh went under in the drenching downpour. In past centuries Bangladesh, a natural disaster–prone area, could count on a flood of that severity only once every fifty years. But since the mid-1900s their number has grown and their severity has intensified. Bangladesh was inundated on average once every four years through the 1970s. In the worst flood of that decade, in 1974, famine killed three hundred thousand people and ignited the revolt that overthrew the nation's founder, Sheik Mujibar Rahman. Since 1980 five "fifty-year" floods have ravaged the country, each worse than the last.

Around the headwaters of the Nile in Ethiopia, above Khartoum, in the region known in biblical times as the "land of milk and honey," a similar chain of events had occurred. A population surge had been followed by extensive tree cutting and poor farming practices, with a result that was depressingly the same.

In the U.S. there was a gathering sense of déjà vu about the torrid summer of 1988 generally. The entire decade of the 1980s had somehow seemed hotter. And indeed it had been. The meteorological records were indicating that the earth's temperature had been growing consistently, alarmingly warmer. The single decade of the 1980s had brought the five hottest summers of the past century. The summer of 1988 was simply the latest, and the hottest—the hottest, on average, since reliable records had been kept beginning in the 1880s. Before 1988 the five warmest years of the last hundred were (in descending order of heat) 1987, 1983, 1981, 1980, and 1986.

The year 1987 had been a particularly worthy precursor to 1988. Drought and famine returned that year to Ethiopia and fifteen other sub-Saharan countries of Africa. There was a period in late October and early November when twelve thousand forest fires burned throughout the southeastern U.S. And that winter was the warmest ever in the north central states. A heat wave swept the Mediterranean, killing more than one thousand people in Greece in a matter of days. Thirty-five million people were afflicted by drought in Africa alone in the first half of the 1980s. Up to a million had died. Tens of millions have been devastated by droughts in India throughout this warmest single decade on record.

Many scientists, looking back through history from this hottest summer of the hottest decade, saw the disturbing truth in yet another light. Since the eighteenth century they had known that certain gases can trap the sun's heat near the earth's surface. That fact had become by the mid-twentieth century one of the most widely accepted principles in the atmospheric sciences. These gases are mainly carbon dioxide, nitrous oxides, methane, tropospheric ozone, and water vapor. When fossil fuels are burned, these gases are released in the combustion process and turned loose in the atmosphere. There they trap the heat in a way similar to the process by which glass traps heat in a greenhouse: They let the light from the sun in but they don't let all the infrared radiation from earth back out. There the heat hangs, captured by the gases. And slowly, gradually, the earth's temperatures rise beyond where they normally would. Scientists have come to call these heat-absorbing gases "greenhouse gases" and the phenomenon they cause the "greenhouse effect."

Beginning with the industrial revolution in the nineteenth century, man began burning fossil fuels—petroleum, coal, oil, and natural gas—at an unprecedented rate and throwing their residues, the greenhouse gases they create, into the atmosphere by the millions of tons annually. Much of the carbon dioxide thus released is taken in by the world's oceans. Some of it is absorbed by the biosphere. But more than half stays airborne in the at-

mosphere. The unavoidable result has been what scientists call the "greenhouse warming" of the planet.

Scientists knew this was happening. But they were not sure—and still aren't—precisely how fast it was happening and what it all meant. But on June 23, 1988, at the height of that oppressive summer, on one of the hottest of those days in Washington, D.C., Dr. James Hansen of the National Aeronautics and Space Administration's Goddard Institute for Space Studies testified at a hearing of the Senate Energy and Natural Resources Committee. He told the Senators what many scientists had been openly speculating and had long believed: Greenhouse warming is here, it is a reality. These scientists believe the earth may soon be warming at a rate of one degree Fahrenheit every decade. To the scientific community, the simple recognition of the arrival of greenhouse warming is freighted with meaning and with enormous potential consequences for all life.

The blazing summer of 1988, the searing droughts in Asia and Africa, Hurricane Gilbert, the devastating floods in the Sudan and Bangladesh, and a serious monsoon failure in India the year before may be only foretastes of what is yet to come as the warming continues.

And that isn't all.

The Hole in the Sky

In 1985, in their understated way, a team of English scientists from the British Antarctic Survey announced in *Nature*, the international science journal, that there was a large hole in the ozone layer above the Antarctic continent. They said it had been recurring there every October since 1977, during the Antarctic spring, shortly after the first sunlight appeared following the cold dark winter. As much as 40 percent of the ozone layer over the continent was being eaten away each spring.

Atmospheric scientists reading the report were stunned. Most of them had never heard of the obscure British research team.

Who were those people anyhow? Were they reliable? Did they realize what they were saying?

It wasn't that scientists were surprised that such a thing was happening—that the ozone layer might be in jeopardy. For a decade a theory had been widely accepted to the effect that CFCs, the compounds released into the atmosphere from the working fluids in air-conditioning systems, the propellants in aerosol cans, and the halons in fire-fighting equipment, might someday reach the stratosphere and eat at the ozone layer. In 1974, in a landmark paper, two chemists in California, Mario Molina and F. Sherwood Rowland, had theorized that the chlorine reaching the stratosphere could conceivably destroy as much as 20 percent of the ozone layer. But nobody expected it would happen first over the Antarctic, and nobody suspected the erosion would be anywhere near as large as the British said it was. If they were right, the ozone layer was eroding in that section of the stratosphere faster, far faster, than the most pessimistic models had predicted.

Many scientists were simply not ready to believe it. The British had used equipment from the 1920s, half a century old. And with these antiquated, ground-based instruments they had measured the lowest concentration of ozone ever recorded in the stratosphere! In point of fact, the British team itself found it hard to believe. They had been patiently measuring the amount of ozone in the atmosphere over Halley Bay in the Antarctic since 1957. And since 1977 they had been watching it diminish every Antarctic spring. They had been sitting on the knowledge all this time because they mistrusted their measurements. But when a second measuring station at the Argentine Islands, one thousand miles to the northwest, began showing the same thing, they decided they had better make their findings public.

Skeptical scientists demanded to know why the sophisticated state-of-the-art monitoring devices aboard the earth satellites hadn't detected a hole that size if it existed. The truth is, the satellites had. The enormous pile of data they had beamed back

simply hadn't been analyzed yet. The keepers of the satellite data rushed to their stored records to see if it was possible the hole could have been overlooked—or worse, noticed, but discounted as preposterous by their computers.

Rummaging rapidly through the data that might have detected so large an ozone loss, the searchers finally found it and gasped. The hole indeed did exist, as the British had said, and it was indeed very large. In 1984 it had been larger than the United States and taller than Mount Everest. The hole was bigger than the Antarctic continent itself. By the spring of 1987, average ozone concentration over the South Pole was down 50 percent, and entirely gone in some spots. And by the spring of 1988, after a group of one hundred scientists from seven countries had intensively reviewed and reanalyzed the data of the past two decades, everybody knew the worst. "Things," said NASA's Robert Watson, "are worse than we thought."

NASA's Donald Heath, the scientist at the Goddard Space Flight Center who was in charge of reviewing the satellite data, said: "We've never seen a drop of this size in history. This is a frightening thing. When you start seeing large changes in ozone where the theory can't account for it, then it raises the question of how good are the model predictions? What are the consequences twenty or fifty years from now if the theory is wrong now?"

What had been happening in the heavens began to become evident to atmospheric chemists. Waiting in the stratosphere over the Antarctic ice mass had been a very conducive set of circumstances—propitious meteorological conditions, the presence of stratospheric clouds, and low concentrations of nitrogen oxides. Into this mix, from earth below, drifted abnormally high concentrations of man-made active CFCs—the Freon from the air conditioners, the halons from the fire-fighting equipment, and the propellants from the aerosol cans. When they reached the stratosphere the sun's intense rays began breaking these intruders down, releasing atoms of chlorine. The chlorine then set in mo-

tion a chain reaction lethal to the fragile ozone layer. It is one of those unfortunate facts of nature that one chlorine molecule in the stratosphere can destroy many thousands of ozone molecules and itself remain unaffected. When the two worlds collided, the chlorine, Pac-man-like, began chewing up the ozone layer.

Two things now seemed depressingly clear. First, the hole couldn't get much deeper than it was; therefore it would very likely spread outward over nearby inhabited parts of the earth, over Argentina, Chile, Brazil, Uruguay, Australia, and New Zealand. Second, such erosion of the precious ozone layer was very likely not uncommon and not limited to southern latitudes. Many eyes turned to the stratosphere above the Arctic. Measurements were made and they tested positive; there was loss of ozone there as well.

The two decades of data collected by the one hundred world scientists and released in 1988 verified the mounting fears. The data showed decreases in the ozone layer of between 1.7 and 3 percent in the summertime and 2.3 to 6.2 percent in the winter across part of the stratosphere above the heavily populated Northern Hemisphere. The trouble is clearly spreading, encompassing virtually all of the U.S. and Europe. And it continues over the Antarctic. The year of heaviest recorded ozone depletion over the frozen continent was 1987. By the end of 1989 the British, still maintaining their watch on the recurring hole in the sky, were reporting an ozone loss as high as it was in that record year.

Since the ozone layer is the only thing lying between earth and sun that keeps out life-menacing ultraviolet rays, the news the British had sprung on the world was very bad indeed. Ozone depletion, treated as theory for the past decade and hotly contested by the CFC producers, was suddenly very real—and very threatening.

Meanwhile, something as real and as threatening was happening closer to the ground.

The Killing Rain

As the invading armada of CFCs continued to tear at the thin ozone shield in the stratosphere, a silent killer was stalking the earth from the lower atmosphere.

Day in and day out, in the Ohio River Valley of the United States, in the industrial complexes of Europe, in China—nearly everywhere that we burn coal and oil to generate the energy to run our twentieth-century world—we are spewing sulfur dioxides into the air through smokestacks and generating plants. And day in and day out in the cities of the world, through the tail pipes of tens of millions of motor vehicles, we are venting tons of nitrogen oxides into the atmosphere.

Some of these sulfur dioxides from industry, SO_2 in technological shorthand, and nitrogen oxides from transportation, NO_x to the scientific world, drop dry to earth in a matter of hours or days at most. But some of them hang in the atmosphere. As they hang, they begin, slowly, insidiously, to oxidize—and to change. The SO_2 changes into sulfuric acid. The NO_x changes into nitric acid. These acids begin to drift slowly away, hugging the lower lining of the atmosphere, riding on the wind currents. Miles away from where they started, sometimes hundreds of miles away, they return to earth, pouring down in the rain, sleet, hail, and snow, setting in with the fog and the mist, or lying gently in with the dew and the frost.

They have become a silent, unseen, killing precipitation. Only their effect is visible. As the hydrogen ions fall to earth they begin, like body snatchers from another planet, to insert themselves in the place of the soil's healthy nutrients—its calcium, magnesium, and potassium. On earth these hydrogen acids mobilize a deadly army of heavy metals, as acids will do. And these mobilized metals—aluminum, cadmium, manganese, mercury, zinc, copper—begin to move through the soil, leaching out, literally kicking out and replacing, the good nutrients.

These acids and their heavy metal allies are killing life. They

are killing fish in the water and trees on the land. The army of metals set in motion by the acids are leaching into the soil, eating at the delicate root systems that supply water to trees and plants, and drifting into lakes and rivers. As the metals undermine from below, other pollutants continue to bombard from above, doing their own kind of damage. Day by day acid rain is pitting protective surfaces; stunting growth, development, and yield; altering species composition of lower life-forms; reducing the population of decomposer organisms; infesting living tissue with metals; undermining reproductive systems; causing skeletal deformities; and ultimately killing.

As the acids and their mobilized metals enter lakes and find that the waters don't have strong alkaline buffering agents to repel them, they gradually choke out all life. If the alkalines in the waters are weak, the acids simply overwhelm, override, and replace them. A heavy snowmelt or a particularly heavy rain can bring with it a temporary surge of acidity that can kill fish by the hundreds.

Here is how a lake dies in the acid rain:

As the acid rain and its heavy metal allies invade, the acid content of the lake rises. The deadly aluminum begins to seep into the gills of the fish in the lake, asphyxiating, then killing them. As the lake's acidity rises, the pH value (the measurement of the acid content of the water) changes. The lower the pH drops, on a scale of 0 to 14, the more uninhabitable the lake becomes. At around 6 pH crustaceans, snails, and mollusks die. Between 6 and 5.5 pH salmon, char, trout, and roach die, followed by sensitive insects and plant and animal plankton. At 5.5 pH whitefish and grayling die. At 5 pH perch and pike die. At 4.5 pH eels die. By then all normal life is gone. White moss has begun to spread over the lake. All that is finally left are insensitive insects and certain invulnerable plant and animal plankton. The lake is dead.

In Sweden, where the effects of acid rain's deadly work was first noticed and earliest felt, more than eighteen thousand lakes

are acidified, four thousand of them grievously so. Fish have died from acid precipitation in more than fifteen hundred lakes and seven Atlantic salmon rivers in southern Norway. Some two hundred lakes in the Adirondack Mountains in the northeastern United States are now considered dead, killed mainly by the acids brought in by the rain from industrial plants in the Ohio River Valley. Some five hundred streams in the mid-Atlantic and southeastern states are showing acid rain damage. In eastern Canada, which gets half of its acid rain from power plants in the United States, a one million square mile area, home to 80 percent of the Canadian population, is threatened by acid rain. More than three hundred thousand Canadian lakes are considered in jeopardy. Half of these are already damaged and more than fourteen thousand are acidified to the point of being uninhabitable for fish. There has been a striking loss of salmon in a score of rivers in Nova Scotia.

The toll is just as heavy on land. Here is how a red spruce tree dies in the acid rain:

The acidic precipitation falls to earth and the acid infests the soil water. The metals mobilized by the acids enter the tree through the fine root filaments. As this is happening the sulfuric acids continue to bombard from the air, and under this double assault the tree is gradually sapped of its vitality. Needles at the top start to turn brown and fall off. Then they begin to shed over the whole tree. Branches begin to break away. The tree top snaps off. Slowly, gradually, the tree dies.

In the autumn of 1983 West Germans opened up their newspapers and turned on their television sets and were stunned. The news said that 34 percent of the nation's trees were yellowing and losing needles or leaves—showing all the symptoms of a forest under siege from acid rain. A more thorough survey the following year found the malaise spreading. Half of West Germany's 18 million acres of forest were reported damaged, including two-thirds of those in the famed Black Forest of southwestern Baden Württemberg. The Germans had a word for

what was happening, a somber, chilling word: *Waldsterben*—forest death. The word, later displaced by a perhaps more accurate but less chilling *neuartige Waldschäden*—literally, new type of forest damage—flew across the country from living room to living room. A poll of West Germans in 1983 showed them more concerned about their dying forests than they were about the Pershing missiles slated to be placed in their country later that year.

Several West German foresters, writing in the *Journal of Forestry*, have editorialized that "Air pollution is now the problem that concerns West German foresters most. The results of two hundred years of forest management seem to be extinguishable within the next ten years. . . . Only a few people think about an all-too-possible scenario: central Europe without forests."

Much of Europe's 336 million acres of forest are reputedly dying under the acid siege. In at least half a dozen countries of central Europe, over a wide swath running through Austria, Czechoslovakia, Luxembourg, the Netherlands, Switzerland, and West Germany, the damage is pervasive; a quarter to half of the forested area is damaged. The lofty Alpine mountain regions of Austria, France, Italy, Switzerland, and West Germany have all been hard hit. In the high elevations of eastern North America, from Canada to the Appalachians, the red spruce forests are suffering serious dieback.

Acid rain is also raking China, the world's largest user of sulfur-creating coal. In Sichuan's thirteen-thousand-acre Maocaoba pine forest, nine trees of every ten have died. In Chongqing (formerly Chungking), forty-five hundred acres of dense Masson pine on Nashan Hill have been reduced by half. Both regions have high acid rain levels. The power plants that are poisoning these forests lack even rudimentary controls. Visitors have reported that each of these plants is surrounded by a circle of desolation over a kilometer wide, where even grass and weeds will no longer grow.

Coal accounts for nearly three-fourths of all energy consumed in China today, and for over 90 percent of all the SO_2 released

in its atmosphere. In 1982 China produced 666 million tons of coal, second only to the United States. By the year 2000, annual coal burning in China is expected to double. Chin Zhiyuan, of China's National Environmental Protection Agency, says that without greater efforts to rein in pollution China may overtake other acid rain countries and "that is not the kind of catching up we want."

Acid rain looms as a rising potential threat now in many other developing countries as well. Large portions of Brazil, southern India, and Southeast Asia are underlain by the types of soils all too familiar in acid-struck parts of the industrial world, the soils most susceptible to acidification.

A disturbing possibility underlies *Waldsterben* wherever in the world that it is occurring. For all the trees that are showing signs of dying, how many are under attack, but not showing it? Researchers at the Virginia Polytechnic Institute, who have documented "hidden injury" in the white pine forests of the Appalachian Mountains, believe it is "highly probable that growth loss in forest subjected to low-level and long-term exposures to air pollutants may be occurring unnoticed and/or underevaluated." In the case of the Appalachians the damage is very likely due to a related problem, regional ozone smog, rather than acid rain.

Where there are as yet no symptoms, neither the extent of the damage nor the outcome are known. Where pollutants remain at relatively low levels, many forest systems will simply continue to absorb them without major damage to the soil, to microorganisms, or to the trees themselves. Yet the silent, killing precipitation continues to work undercover, adding bit by bit to the chronic stress, day by day and year by year. Going on out of sight is a staged decline that in extreme cases could end in complete ecosystem collapse.

The forest death spreading through central Europe today could be the beginning of such a train of events on a broad scale. Even if pollution remains at today's levels, forests and soils continually

exposed to this degree of slow stress may in time simply lose their resistance. Moreover, long before the ecosystem collapses, other resources that depend on a healthy, well-functioning forest will be affected.

The killing of lakes and forests is only part of the legacy of acid rain. We have compelling testimony now that it can also kill people. Four eminent physicians from the American Academy of Pediatrics, the American Lung Association, the American Public Health Association, and New York's Mount Sinai Medical Center testified before a U.S. Senate committee in 1987 that acid rain is a menace to human health. In their professional opinions, based upon their experience, the threat to human health was now sufficient to justify, and they unanimously recommended, legislation to control SO_2 and NO_x emissions. Their testimony added an entirely new dimension to the acid rain debate. Before that it had focused on surface waters primarily and damage to forests.

Acid precipitation is intruding as well on groundwater supplies, invading wells, and leaching into drinking water systems around the world. It is even scarring and pitting the symbols of our cultural life. Calcite, a major component of marble, sandstone, and other construction materials, is particularly susceptible to acid rain. No monument is safe if it lies in the path of acid precipitation. The Washington Monument and the White House in Washington; the Field Museum of Natural History in Chicago; the Acropolis and the Parthenon in Athens; Trajan's Column in Rome; the historic Jewish cemetery in Prague; the Cologne, Freiburg, and Ulm cathedrals; castles on the Rhine— all have been pitted by acids from the atmosphere. In India, the Taj Mahal now lies in the path of sulfur dioxides from a new oil refinery only thirty miles upwind.

Liable to attack are unprotected carbon steel, zinc, galvanized steel, aluminum material, stainless steel, plastics, paper, glass, paint, masonry, leather, textiles, plaster, and electrical contacts —virtually all of the building blocks of our modern prosperity. The same acids are also behind much of the regional haze that

is clouding visibility in some of our once pristine national parks. The Shenandoah National Park, Arches, Mesa Verde, the Grand Canyon, Bryce, Canyonlands, the Petrified Forest, Sequoia-Kings, the Great Smokies—all have been shrouded at one time or another in acid haze.

It is difficult to pinpoint exactly the cost of the damage that acid rain is doing. But the experts have offered estimates. One of these puts the annual cost in the United States alone at more than $5 billion—$2 billion in damage to materials, $1.75 billion to forest ecosystems, $1 billion to agriculture, $250 million to aquatic ecosystems, and $100 million in general damages.

But the menace of acid rain can't be measured in dollars alone. More important is what it does to quality of life. The matter is a very personal one with me, because the region of the U.S. hardest hit by acid rain has been the Northeast, that part of the country where I was raised and which we all thought invulnerable to the pollution settling in over more heavily populated, industrialized parts of the country. It has shown us that no region is spared by the environmental Four Horsemen, that these grim riders are apt to strike anywhere.

Nor can dollars alone measure the true cost of the holocaust that is now occurring elsewhere on earth, in the great tropical rain forests of the world, the richest sanctuaries of life ever to inhabit the globe.

Trouble in the Rain Forest

Deep in Brazil's Amazon, the year 1987 is remembered as a year of fire. Satellites monitoring the outbreak of fires in the lush, life-teeming rain forest from June to October, the dry season in the Amazon, counted 350,000 of them—more than a thousand a day, since the burning season is but five months long. These fires can burn for twenty-four to forty-eight hours, therefore some of them may have been counted more than once. But even so, by conservative estimate, 170,000 fires raged in the Amazon that summer. On the worst day, September 9, the satellite counted

7,603 of them. By the end of 1987 an area of rain forest the size of Austria had been burned to the ground. These fires were not set by accident; the humid, moist rain forest isn't given to natural fires. They were set by human hands.

It is happening constantly, at a pace difficult to comprehend. In the time it takes you to read this thirty-word sentence another seven acres of tropical forests will have been burned or bulldozed from the face of the earth.

Unlike that silent stalker, acid rain, deforestation—the fourth major menace in the quartet of global forces wreaking unwanted change in the world environment—is something immediately visible. It is happening in plain sight, out there for everybody to see, lending depressing reality to the environmental axiom that forests precede nations and deserts follow them.

The Smithsonian Institution's Thomas Lovejoy has called the Amazon "a library for life sciences, the world's greatest pharmaceutical laboratory and a flywheel of climate." This greatest of the rain forests covers nearly three million square miles, an area nearly as large as the entire United States. It spans nine South American countries from Brazil in the east to Peru in the west, and from Venezuela in the north to Bolivia in the south.

Dense life-teeming flywheels of climate such as these once girdled the equatorial midsection of the globe in stunning profusion from South America to Africa to Malaysia to Indonesia. The rain forests store carbon, the parent element of the preeminent greenhouse gas, for photosynthesis. They bottle up within themselves—and withhold from the atmosphere—billions of tons of carbon dioxide (CO_2), enough of it to play a central role in keeping the world's climate in a state of relative equilibrium. As the Third World, where most of these great forests have lain for centuries, has continued to swell in population, the forests have begun to go, by the millions of acres. As they go, they emit their billions of tons of stored CO_2 into the atmosphere, adding massively to the greenhouse warming. And as they go, they take with them to extinction uncounted numbers of living species.

The rain forests, with all their variety of life and their seventy-

five billion tons of stored carbon, are a priceless, fragile necessity for the planet. And they are being torched into oblivion, every fire magnifying the greenhouse effect. It has been going on a long time. Twenty million acres of Amazon forest were razed for cattle pasture between 1966 and 1968. In Asia, more than four million acres of rain forest were lost between 1976 to 1980. Almost six million acres of tropical forests were destroyed every year in Africa between 1980 and 1985. Latin America and Southeast Asia have lost two-fifths of their rain forests. By 1980 the world had lost 40 percent of its once grand total—nearly half.

And the destruction goes on, gathering momentum. In 1988 alone 50,000 square miles of the Amazon rain forest in Brazil, an area as big as Louisiana, were burned and stripped away. The pace of obliteration worldwide is breakneck—nearly an acre every second, 54 acres every minute, 3,240 acres every hour, 77,760 acres every day, 28 million acres every year. The world is on a pace to lose them all by sometime early in the next century.

The world's precious wetlands, too, are being drained beyond redemption. In the forty-eight continental United States, in the two decades between 1950 and 1970, nine million acres of wetlands gave way to farming, urban growth, and vacation developments. The destruction continues at a rate of a million acres a year. More than half of all the wetlands in the continental United States have been destroyed. Forty percent of those in Canada have vanished. More than a third of the world's endangered animal species depend for their existence on these disappearing havens of life.

As the forests and wetlands go, the deserts, lifeless and incapable of shielding us from catastrophic global warming, come—at a clip of fifteen million new acres a year. An area the size of the state of West Virginia is lost beyond hope of reclamation every year. Another fifty million acres every year become too debilitated to support profitable farming or grazing. Hundreds of millions of acres are moving along that barren path. The United Nations Environmental Program estimates that eleven

billion acres—an area the size of Africa, 35 percent of the earth's land surface containing one-fifth of all of its people—are now threatened by desertification.

For a nation, particularly a developing nation, its natural resources are its capital. And over the past two decades that capital has been slipping away, alarmingly. Forty years ago 30 percent of Ethiopia was covered by forests. Twelve years ago it was down to 4 percent. Today it may be 1 percent. India's forests at the turn of this century covered as much as 40 percent of the country. Today they cover but 14 percent and are disappearing daily.

The pattern by which vegetated and productive land is turned into a barren landscape is depressingly the same. For centuries the vegetation—a forest, a savannah, a grassland—has successfully held back the desert. But then people begin to need the land the vegetation covers. They move in and begin to clear it for their herds and their crops. They strip the trees for fuelwood. And slowly the sands begin to move, shifting in, filling in, pushing back. And eventually the sandstorms come.

This process has repeated itself with a vengeance in Mauritania in the sub-Sahara. Herdsmen in that pastoral country, one of the poorest in the world, overgrazed their herds in the central and southern regions, stripping bare the vegetation that held back the sand. And at the same time there was drought, which exacerbates the desertification process. The Sahara inexorably began marching in. There were only 43 sandstorms in Mauritania in the 1960s. In the 1970s there were ten times as many. By 1983 there were 240 in one year. As the land became impoverished, so did the people on it.

Desertification is now well under way over much of Africa's drought-stricken Sahelian zone, across a band of countries south of the Sahara that stretches from Senegal and Mauritania on the African west coast to Chad and parts of the Sudan to the east. Seven nations with thirty-one million inhabitants have been particularly hard hit—Mauritania, Burkina Faso, Chad, Gambia, Mali, Nigeria, and Senegal.

Like the Germans, peasants in western Nigeria have a word

for what has happened, just as chilling in its description of desertification as *Waldsterben* is in its description of acid rain: *laabu, y bu*—the land is dead.

The inexorable march of the desert, fueled by the twenty-year drought that has gripped the Sahel, has pushed Mauritania's two million people into an ever-shrinking strip of still habitable coastal land. Only 0.2 percent of Mauritania's 386,000 square miles is arable today. No nation in the Sahel has less. The average, even for Mauritania's desert-threatened Sahelian neighbors, is 8 percent. As Mauritania's traditional roving pastoral population of herdsmen has been driven before the encroaching desert, it has streamed into a narrow patch of towns and cities dominated by a burgeoning Nouakchott on the Atlantic shore. Predominantly rural in 1965 when the desert began to move in, Mauritania is now 85 percent urban. Nouakchott has exploded, from a town with a population of 20,000 in 1960 to a bulging city of more than 350,000 today, half of that number refugees fleeing from the advancing desert.

The sands of the Sahara will continue to march over Mauritania until somehow vegetation is restored and the dunes are again fixed in place as they had been for centuries before—if indeed it is not too late for that. Meanwhile the sand continues to shift and move and sift in. It has now covered whole villages and agricultural fields. Schools, mosques, and oases have been abandoned. The ancient Mauritanian cities of Chinguetti, Tichett, Oualata, and Ouadane are under running siege from the sand. The dunes have piled up now to glacial heights even over the nation's vital main artery, the Highway of Hope. Today much hope has been sapped from Mauritania by the drifting sand and the lifeless desert.

The merciless Sahara is also now beginning to work its devastation north of the parched Sahel in Algeria, Egypt, Libya, Morocco, and Tunisia, where escalating human and cattle populations have begun to exceed the capacity of the land to support them.

* * *

As the encroaching deserts represent lifelessness, their opposites, the retreating rain forests and wetlands, represent life. Although they only cover 7 percent of the earth's surface, the rain forests contain at least half of the earth's species. An acre in the life-rich Brazilian rain forest can contain as many as 60 different species of trees. In its entire expanse, North America has only 700 different native tree species. A four-square-mile swatch of the Amazon surveyed by the National Academy of Sciences in 1982 held 750 separate tree species, 125 different mammal species, 400 bird species, 100 different kinds of reptiles, and 60 species of amphibians. Each type of tree, it was calculated, supported as many as 400 separate insect species.

Harvard University's Edward O. Wilson, the world expert on the diversity of species, tells us in a recent article in *Scientific American*:

> Every tropical biologist has stories of the prodigious variety in this one habitat type. From a single leguminous tree in Peru, I once retrieved forty-three ant species belonging to twenty-six genera, approximately equal to the ant diversity of all of the British Isles. In ten selected one-hectare (2.47 acre) plots in Kalimantan in Indonesia, Peter S. Ashton of Harvard University found more than seven hundred tree species, about equal to the number of tree species native to all North America. The current world record at this writing (certain to be broken) was established in 1988 by Alwyn H. Gentry of the Missouri Botanical Garden, who identified approximately three hundred tree species in each of two one-hectare plots near Iquitos, Peru.

The list of products for man's use that are drawn from these teeming reservoirs of life is virtually limitless. From them we get many of our basic industrial and pharmaceutical products: exudates, gums, latexes, resins, tannins, steroids, waxes, esters, acids, phenols, alcohols, essential oils, edible oils, rattans, bamboo, flavorings, sweeteners, spices, balsams, pesticides, and dye stuffs. Out of these we make foods, medicines, polishes, sedatives, cos-

metics, and golf balls. Embedded in the rain forests are hosts of potential compounds of unbounded benefit to man. The piquia tree, for instance, produces a compound that is toxic to leaf cutter ants, which cause millions of dollars of damage each year to South American agriculture. There could be many other living, self-regenerating raw materials deep in the forest that could do the work of dangerous synthetic pesticides. Other forest chemicals have proven antipathetic to many of humankind's worst enemies—among them cancer and hypertension.

One of every four pharmaceuticals made into medicines by Western chemists comes from a tropical plant. The cup of coffee for breakfast, the banana for an afternoon snack, the cinnamon and nutmeg that spice the dinner dessert, the kid's rubber ball, the glue for the airplane model, the latex paint on the walls, the anesthesia to ease the pain of surgery—they all come from the rain forest. The list goes on and on. The rain forest left standing is far more valuable to us all than the field, the pasture, or the road that is replacing it.

Perhaps the only species not gladly encompassed by the rain forests is their two hundred million human inhabitants. Even most of those, however, people indigenous to the forest, have learned, like all the other life, to live in a degree of harmony with it and to use it without destroying it. People native to the forest have long understood that it is far more valuable alive than dead. Yet even this kind of human being, who conforms to it rather than deforming it, has, like other life in the forest, become a threatened species.

Chico Mendes was one of them. He is today extinct. Mendes was a mustachioed, black-haired native of the Brazilian Amazon with a ready smile, a beautiful wife, and two young children. He took up the cause of the forest because he wanted to save the way of life and the livelihood of the rubber tappers, or *seringueiros*, in the western state of Acre. Acre's forest was still mostly intact, only 4 percent of it gone. But it too was in jeopardy, as ranchers continued to expand their holdings and raze more forest. This

sparked a series of bloody clashes between the ranchers and the *seringueiros*, who were harvesters of latex and Brazil nuts.

Mendes was a leader of the *seringueiros*. He helped convince the Inter-American Development Bank to suspend funding temporarily for further paving of the road between Rondônia and Acre, for it is down such roads that development comes to the rain forest. Mendes and his men tried to dissuade the peasants in the forest from clearing their land. As a result, he became a marked man, surviving one assassination attempt after another. In 1988 he and two hundred *seringueiros* peaceably turned back a rancher who wanted to cross land claimed by rubber tappers to cut an adjacent three hundred-acre plot. The death threats grew more frequent. Finally, in December that year he was gunned down as he stepped out of his doorway. It is uncertain how long the *seringueiros* can now survive in the face of the irresistible drive to torch and clear the rain forests.

How did all of these things happen? What has turned loose these destructive elements on earth? What has brought the warming world, the eroding ozone layer, and the acid rain? What has set the rain forests in retreat and the deserts in motion? The answer is clear.

4

How It Happened

Walt Kelly's ungrammatical comic strip character, Pogo, spoke for all ages of humanity when he uttered this philosophical truth: "We has met the enemy and it is us." While it has been the truth about "us" down through time, it was never more true than in the case of our present environmental crisis. It is us—humankind—who have loosed these Four Horsemen of the coming climatic apocalypse on ourselves. It is us who are burning all those fossil fuels and pouring all those greenhouse gases into our own atmosphere. It is us who are ripping those holes in the fragile ozone layer with our CFCs and halons. It is us who are sending the acids from our smokestacks and tail pipes into our lakes and forests. It is us who are stripping our planet of its life-sustaining tropical forests and wetlands. It is us who have conducted the heedless four-decade chemical experiment on our planet that has all but set our air on fire. It is us who are playing these two ends against the middle: burning the fossil fuels that throw greenhouse gases into the atmosphere, even as we strip away the earth's capacity to absorb them as nature intended.

Speaking during a U.S. Senate committee hearing, Columbia University geochemist Wallace Broecker put it a little differently

from Pogo, but his meaning was the same: "The inhabitants of Planet Earth are quietly conducting a gigantic environmental experiment. So vast and so sweeping will be the impact of this experiment that, were it brought before any responsible council for approval, it would be firmly rejected as having potentially dangerous consequences. Yet, the experiment goes on with no significant interference from any jurisdiction or nation."

The situation is full of sad ironies. We—mainly the industrialized nations—have become the Prometheus of the twentieth century, destroying our own habitat. The Prometheus of Greek mythology stole fire from the gods and gave it to man, and Zeus chained him to a mountain where he was lashed by the seas and burned by the sun. We have stolen the fire of fossil fuels and have invited the same general consequences. We are already paying the price in personal and environmental health.

The day we began burning fossil fuels at such mindless rates to make our homes and our environment more habitable, we began turning our earth into an uninhabitable hothouse. The day we started air-conditioning and refrigerating ourselves, our cars, our buildings, and our food, and spraying everything with our aerosol cans, we began unwittingly ripping holes in the ozone layer that shields us from harm. As we began cooling ourselves, we began setting the world on fire. As we began enriching our lives, we began killing other life and impoverishing the lives of Erics and Luisas yet unborn.

Between the Hot and the Cold

Planet Earth doesn't travel alone. It wheels through the solar system between two very radical companions, Venus and Mars. No associates could be more different from earth and from each other. Venus is so hot that it would boil the blood of any human who entered its sphere. Mars is so cold that a human visitor would instantly freeze. Venus is hot because its atmosphere is composed largely of carbon dioxide, which traps heat. Mars is

cold because it has almost no CO_2—or any other greenhouse gas—and traps very little heat. There is no known life on either planet. Earth has managed to strike a delicate, life-sustaining balance between these two extremes on either side. It has had just the proper mixture of the greenhouse gases in its makeup down through the millennia—not too much and not too little. It has therefore nurtured and protected life.

But over the last century, and particularly over the past four decades, earth's most advanced form of life—us—has engaged in activities that are now dangerously disrupting this delicate balance of not too much or too little CO_2. We have done it by burning fossil fuels; our reliance on them amounts to an addiction. We have done it by slashing and burning the rain forests. We have done it with intensive agricultural practices. We have done it with a population explosion. And we have done it with chemicals.

A prophetic Swedish chemist named Svante Arrhenius saw much of this coming in 1896. He warned us. In that year he proposed a theory that coal, oil, and natural gas—fossil fuels—emit CO_2 as the basic by-product of their combustion. He warned then that this was leading us into trouble. It was clear to him that the inevitable rapid leap in the use of coal in the coming decades would raise CO_2 concentrations in the atmosphere. And this was going to raise global temperatures.

For half a century few people paid much attention to Arrhenius's theory. The temperature didn't get appreciably warmer. So the theory gathered cobwebs in the scientific literature, until it was resurrected by a study by the Scripps Institution of Oceanography half a century later. The Scripps findings suggested that half of the CO_2 released by burning fossil fuels was being permanently trapped in the earth's atmosphere. Could Arrhenius have been right? The scientific world needed hard evidence. So a CO_2 measuring station was set up on Mauna Loa volcano, and a young Scripps graduate student named Charles D. Keeling, who was destined to become a pioneer researcher in the field,

was sent there for an extended period to measure the air in the pollution-free mid-Pacific. Keeling's data from Mauna Loa over the past three decades have proved revelatory. They have recorded a rise in CO_2 from 315 parts per million in the 1950s to over 350 parts per million in the 1980s—an abnormal 10 percent increase. Nature alone could not have done it. It had to have help from the human race.

How abnormal is 10 percent? Measurements from air bubbles trapped in the cores of glacial ice tell us that this modest-sounding increase has taken the concentration of CO_2 in the atmosphere higher than it has been in 160,000 years. Follow-up data from global circulation models have since proved Arrhenius was a prophet—and a bearer, it turns out, of very bad news. The news may be worse than anybody at first thought. Earth is not only heating up, but may be heating up at a faster rate than Arrhenius and his successors predicted. (In recent months some scientists have been questioning this; they now think the warming isn't going to be as high, after all, as they first feared. But that is by no means a unanimous opinion.)

We began pumping CO_2 from fossil fuels into the atmosphere in earnest in the mid-nineteenth century. In 1860, on the eve of the American Civil War and at the beginning of our industrial revolution, human beings were adding just over 90 million tons a year into the atmosphere. Today they pour CO_2 into the air in unconstrained profusion, at a rate of 5.5 billion tons annually, more than a ton for every person on earth. Over that century and a third humankind has dumped 185 billion tons of carbon dioxide into the atmosphere, the better part of it since the 1950s. This man-made outpouring of CO_2 is responsible for half of the warming to which the earth is now committed.

Before we began turning free this vast volume of fossil carbon it had rested inertly in the ground for hundreds of millions of years, safely sequestered by the earth's normal carbon cycles. Now each year, in a burning without parallel in history, we are in effect restoring unthinkable quantities of carbon back into the atmo-

sphere that had taken plants millions of years to remove. Newly set free in the atmosphere, the CO_2 is overwhelming the capacity of the biosphere and the oceans to absorb it. And therein lies the crisis.

Because of its sheer majority, CO_2 is the world environment's leading menace. But it may not even be the worst of Arrhenius's bad news. The worst may yet come from some of the other greenhouse gases—methane, nitrous oxide, and earth ozone— which together with CFCs are responsible for the other 50 percent of the warming to which the world is already committed. Some of these other greenhouse gases are far more pervasive, powerful, and vicious than CO_2. They have been growing steadily in influence. They must somehow be brought under control. For a century, from 1880 to 1980, CO_2 contributed two-thirds of all the greenhouse gases in the atmosphere. Methane was a distant second at 15 percent. CFCs were at 8 percent. Nitrous oxide trailed at 2 percent. In the 1980s these grim outriders, as a group, have caught up to CO_2.

Methane (CH_4) is a low order of gas that drifts into the atmosphere largely from bacterial decomposition of organic matter. It rises from the dregs—from landfills, from the biological wastes of ruminants, from decaying plants and trees, rice paddies, trash dumps, and human sewage. Its natural sources are mainly wetlands, wild animals, and termites. Methane is now responsible for nearly 20 percent of earth's warming. Analyses of air trapped in the polar ice tell us that the levels of methane in the atmosphere began rising around the year 1600, at about the time Shakespeare was writing *Hamlet*. Its levels since have doubled, and its role in the warming equation enlarges by 1 to 2 percent every year. Deforestation is believed to have contributed to methane's striking increase in the atmosphere over the past decade. By 2030 this gas could be increasing global warming by as much as 40 percent.

Nitrous oxide (N_2O) is a colorless, sweet-smelling compound that chemists, without humor, sometimes call laughing gas. Some

of the man-made increase of this villain gas, known to produce euphoria and mirth when inhaled, comes from nitrogen fertilizers and biomass burning. Some comes from fossil fuel combustion. Loose in the atmosphere it produces no mirth. It is 250 times more potent than CO_2 and hangs on in the atmosphere infinitely longer—for one hundred to two hundred years. Its relative concentration in the atmosphere has tripled over the past century. Even so, it is only one thousandth as common as CO_2. But its enormous longevity means that even after we have devised a way to treat it, we may have to wait a century or more to see any effect.

Tropospheric ozone(O_3), identical to its benign counterpart in the stratosphere but lying close to earth, is another potent greenhouse gas well-known as a major cause of smog and a companion to acid rain. It accounts for 5 to 7 percent of the earth's warming. Created by automobiles and other human industrial activities, its share of the blame for global warming is also on the rise annually.

The CFCs are chemicals, but in the atmosphere they act like a greenhouse gas. They are as potent at blocking heat as any of the others, now contributing nearly 17 percent of the earth's warming caused by humans, and growing fastest of all.

These, then, are the major greenhouse gases and their accomplices. They are not, however, the only fossil fuel pollutants humankind is pumping into the atmosphere. Every year worldwide we also generate millions of tons of sulfur dioxide, particulate matter, oxides of nitrogen, carbon monoxide, and hydrocarbons. It has been said that the repertoire of fossil-fuel pollutants we now emit into the air is not only wrecking the environment, but may be prematurely killing as many as fifty thousand people in the U.S. alone every year.

These gases have always been with us. And human activity has always altered the environment in one way or the other. So why in the past century or so has it become such a problem? Why now?

When the twentieth century began, neither human numbers

nor technology had the power to radically alter planetary systems for good or evil. But as the century nears its close, we now possess numbers and technologies powerful enough to alter the environment on a global scale. Indeed, we now have both the numbers and the technology to destroy the world, to impose cataclysmic changes on its land, its waters, its atmosphere, its stratosphere, and all its life forms. And the world's elite, the industrialized nations, have been behind most of it. They generate 75 percent of all the greenhouse gases that are being poured into the atmosphere.

Environmentally, the last century and a half could be called the Fossil Fuel Age. In this age, and primarily since 1950, the use of fossil fuels has multiplied nearly thirtyfold. Industrial production, the reason for it all, has multiplied by fifty times. The yearly increase of production today is as large as the total production in Europe at the end of the 1930s. Into every year now, we jam the decades of industrial growth—and environmental disruption—that formed the basis of the entire prewar European economy.

Synthetic chemical production, a revolution unto itself, has also spun out of control. Some seventy thousand to eighty thousand chemicals are now on the market—and in the environment. Another one thousand to two thousand new ones enter each year. Most of them go on sale without anybody knowing what they will do to the environment and the biosphere today, tomorrow, or years from now. No toxicity data exists for eight of every ten chemicals used in commercial products and processes inventoried under the U.S. Toxic Substances Control Act. Human beings—and all life—are exposed to these thousands of chemicals in the air we breathe, the water we drink, and the food we eat. Nobody knows for sure what they are doing to us. But many of them are known to be highly toxic and dangerously harmful to human health.

That birth defects or cancer caused by exposure to these chemicals may not show up for years—even for decades—is not re-

assuring. By then the damage they have done can't be undone. It is the same for all of nature. Like the human body, animals, plants, forests—and the climate—may absorb stress for long periods without outward sign of damage. Then suddenly the harm strikes full force and becomes distressingly evident.

As Rachel Carson said nearly three decades ago in *Silent Spring*, the chemicals to which life is asked to make its adjustment today are "no longer merely the calcium and silica and copper and all the rest of the minerals washed out of the rocks and carried in rivers to the sea." They are another matter altogether. They are "the synthetic creations of man's inventive mind, brewed in his laboratories, and having no counterparts in nature. To adjust to these chemicals would require time on the scale that is nature's; it would require not merely the years of a man's life but the life of generations."

And even adjustment, were it possible, would be futile in the long term, "for the new chemicals come from our laboratories in an endless stream; almost five hundred annually [far more today] find their way into actual use in the United States alone. The figure is staggering and its implications are not easily grasped—five hundred new chemicals to which the bodies of men and animals are required somehow to adapt each year, chemicals totally outside the limits of biologic experience."

This chemical hemorrhage has in no way subsided in the three decades since Carson wrote those angry words. Nor have the implications.

Our headlong plunge into the industrial and chemical revolutions has been without foresight and planning. Zimbabwe's Victoria Chitepo told the World Commission on Environment and Development in 1986:

The remarkable achievements of the celebrated Industrial Revolution are now beginning seriously to be questioned principally because the environment was not considered at the time. It was felt that the sky was so vast and clear nothing could ever change

its color, our rivers so big and their water so plentiful that no amount of human activity could ever change their quality, and there were trees and natural forests so plentiful that we will never finish them. After all, they grow again. Today we should know better.

Perhaps we should have known better about CFCs as well. But they fooled us with their benign dispositions for nearly half a century.

Jekyll and Hyde

F. Sherwood Rowland in 1973 was just rounding into his tenth year as the head of the chemistry department at the University of California at Irvine. He had a promising group of researchers in his stable of young postdoctoral chemists, and none was more promising than Mario Molina, an ambassador's son from Mexico. Neither Molina, who was a photochemist, nor Rowland, who was a radiochemist, knew much about atmospheric chemistry. But the two hit on a research project that would have Molina tracing the whereabouts of chlorofluorocarbons in the atmosphere.

The two chemists made a contrasting pair. Rowland was six feet five inches tall, with a booming voice and a reputation in chemical research befitting his height. Molina was thin, slight of build, soft-spoken, young, and scholarly, a relative newcomer to the discipline. He set out to track the CFCs with his accustomed thoroughness, educating himself in the library on the finer points of atmospheric chemistry as he went along.

The young researcher followed the trail of the compounds into the stratosphere. Lying out there between thirteen and thirty-five miles above the earth, as everybody knew, was a gossamer web of ozone no more substantial than a piece of tissue paper. But that gauzy layer of ozone was the only substance between sun and earth that kept out ultraviolet light, which in too great a volume can genetically alter and even kill life. It was also known

that the chlorine in CFCs could turn ozone to impotent molecules of oxygen—in effect eating it up.

Molina began toting up figures on a calculator and jotting them down on a pad. The more he added and the more he wrote, the less he believed what he was seeing. So he added the figures again—and again. They kept coming up with the same answers. This was more than he could handle. He had to see Rowland. Rowland added the figures, then added them again, and was as stunned as Molina. What the figures kept telling the two chemists was that if the CFCs kept flooding the stratosphere at 1973 levels, between 7 and 13 percent of the ozone layer would be depleted within the next century—enough to seriously alter life on earth.

After much agonizing and rechecking and consultation with other chemists they respected, Rowland and Molina went public with these figures in June 1974 in a paper for *Nature*. Even after it was published they continued to work with the unbelievable figures. The more they worked, the worse the figures looked. They showed that if CFC production continued to escalate as it was doing, at 10 percent a year, until 1990 and remained steady thereafter, 5 to 7 percent of the ozone layer would be destroyed by 1995 and 30 to 50 percent would be gone by 2050. The message was clear: CFCs must be banned as soon as possible. It was something the $8 billion United States CFC industry didn't want to hear.

There followed a fifteen-year struggle in which Rowland and Molina had continuously to defend their findings against attack from the industry. But the figures continued to stand up. Then, in 1985, the diffident chemists from the obscure British Antarctic survey reported the hole in the ozone layer over the Antarctic. Since then it has generally been agreed that CFCs are an undeniable menace to the environment and must go.

The consequences of the chemical revolution are nowhere more vividly illustrated than in the CFCs that are ripping holes in the stratospheric ozone. Their concentrations in our environment

have been growing faster than any other greenhouse gas, at a rate of about 5 percent a year. These compounds, which are such scourges in the stratosphere, act in unholy league with the other greenhouse gases in the atmosphere. (The assault on the environment is a team effort. The Four Horsemen ride together.) Pound for pound the CFCs are ten thousand times more potent than CO_2 in their ability to trap heat and prevent it from radiating back into space.

The environmental upside of these synthetic compounds, if there could be said to be one, is that being wholly man-made, CFCs are also the easiest to bring under control. The worldwide effort to do so has progressed, since the British discovered the ozone hole over the Antarctic, faster than any other preventive effort now underway.

When contained on earth, the CFCs and halons are among the most benign of chemicals. They can do wonderful things. No class of chemicals has brought people greater comfort. They are also known as chlorines and bromines. And in the industrial world they are known by numbers—CFC-11 and CFC-12 being the most common, accounting for 80 percent of all CFCs produced. From them comes the Freon that has made our homes, businesses, and cars habitable in the increasingly hot summer months. They have helped us fight fires more efficiently. They are the blowing agents that have made our furniture cushions thicker, our carpets plusher, our insulation tighter, and our car seats softer. In these CFCs is the magic from which has been devised aerosol sprays for everything—for our furniture, for our bodies, for our hair. These compounds have been turned into the wonder solvents that have conquered the toughest of dirts and stains and made possible the computer revolution. The chlorines and bromines and their kind have built a rich and powerful economic empire within our economy. The end-use value of installed equipment and products carrying them is estimated at $135 billion. In the United States, the world's leading maker and user of CFCs, these wonder chemicals have put one hundred

million refrigerators into our kitchens; they air-condition ninety million of our cars and one hundred thousand of our buildings.

But CFCs and halons are only benign when they are in air conditioners, in fire-fighting equipment, in cushions, or in cans. When they escape, as they do in frightful volume, they drift slowly up—it takes them six to eight years or longer—to the stratosphere. There, their work is not making our lives easier and more comfortable. Their work is to devastate the ozone layer. And they can survive to do that dirty work for as long as a century. With every pool of discarded Freon and with every misty spray from an aerosol can, their army of destruction is reinforced and grows more malignant. And halons, which so effectively quench destructive fire on earth, literally wreak destruction in the stratosphere.

We are helpless now to stop the host of CFCs and halons that have already escaped. Those that haven't yet arrived at the stratosphere are on their way. Another two million tons of them are trapped in foams, appliances, air conditioners and fire-fighting equipment on earth, awaiting their freedom and their run at the ozone layer.

Concentrations of chlorine in the upper atmosphere have grown from 0.6 parts per billion to 2.7 parts per billion in the past quarter century—a whopping increase. They are expected to triple by 2075. Bromines are expected to grow even faster—tenfold from their current 1 percent level. All this will happen no matter what we do now. It is too late to stop these even if we were to freeze all worldwide production and consumption of them today. Our children and their children, and many of us in our old age, are clearly in for it. The best that we can do now is to stop using them, and to do that as soon as possible.

The British discovery of the hole in the ozone shield, which so convincingly verified the stunning figures compiled by Rowland and Molina, has in effect ended the brief reign of CFCs on earth, if not in the stratosphere.

In the autumn of 1984, Rowland, weary from ten long years of waging the ozone wars, despaired of CFCs ever being ban-

ished. "From what I've seen over the past ten years," he told an interviewer, "nothing will be done about this problem until there is further evidence that a significant loss of ozone has occurred. Unfortunately, this means that if there is a disaster in the making in the stratosphere we are probably not going to avoid it."

The following May the British went public with their findings over the Antarctic and made a prophet of Rowland.

"The hole," Rowland says, "changed everything. It got the governments to believe there is a problem." It catapulted the CFC issue into the status of an emergency, where it belonged. It made the Hyde side of the CFC Jekyll personality plainly evident. These handy chemicals are bound to be replaced now by alternative compounds. They must be.

It may be much harder, however, displacing the gases that are causing the problem nearer earth.

The Chilling Couplet

Acid rain has had many aliases—none of them complimentary. "The silent crisis," "an ongoing environmental catastrophe," "a boundless threat to our environment," "an unpremeditated form of chemical warfare," "a chemical leprosy" have all been employed to describe this menace. A Swedish minister of agriculture has said, doubtless from firsthand experience, that it can appear "frightening, elusive, and unstoppable."

The chilling couplet, "acid rain," was first uttered by an English chemist, Robert Angus Smith, in 1872 in an extraordinary book, *Air and Rain: The Beginnings of a Chemical Climatology*. In it he refined two decades of close observations around Manchester into a theory of the problem and the mechanics of acid rain as we now know it. He was astonishingly near the mark. Even before Smith, as far back as 1661, scientists were noting and remarking on the migration of polluting particles and smoke and the presence of sulfur in dew and falling rain. Smith brought it all together and tried to explain it.

But few listened. Fewer still commented. Three-quarters of a

century later, in the 1950s, Eville Gorham, a young Canadian ecologist studying in Smith's England, built another major bridge to our understanding of acid rain and how it works. Still the scientific world was little moved. I know how it is. For the better part of a decade in the U.S. Senate, through most of the 1980s, I tried to pass meaningful legislation to curb this menace. I have also had trouble getting people to listen and act.

Appropriately, the definitive unmasking of the acid rain threat came from Sweden, where it first surfaced as a major problem. In the late 1960s Svante Oden, a Swedish scientist, undertook to unify all the knowledge about acid precipitation. He produced a set of unconventional ideas and a big scientific commotion. He broke the bad news that acid precipitation was a large-scale regional phenomenon throughout much of Europe, that rain and surface waters were becoming ever more acidic, that sulfur and nitrogen acids were traveling long distances across national borders, and that the acid deposition fluctuated with the seasons. And he accurately detailed the damage it was doing.

He woke everybody up. Suddenly scientists from three disciplines—limnology (the study of freshwater lakes), agriculture, and atmospheric chemistry—were scrambling to see what Oden was talking about. The debate he triggered still rages.

The origin and dynamics of acid rain are simple enough: Fossil fuel combustion in power plants and automobiles produces oxides of sulfur and nitrogen, which after a few days aloft in the atmosphere begin to convert to acids, called hydrogen ions. In that state they travel long distances, reducing visibility where they go, and ultimately settle on the ground and in water across large regions of the world. It is happening everywhere, this migration of this silent killer from the cities to the lakes and forests. Between 1900 and 1985 the world's annual sulfur dioxide emissions increased sixfold. Nitrogen oxide emissions multiplied ten times over. And with them, the crisis they cause has escalated around the world. Sixty million tons of sulfur dioxide are thrown into the air annually in Europe, including the Soviet Union.

Eighty percent of it is from the combustion of fossil fuels and 20 percent from various industrial processes. In North America, thirty-two million tons of SO_2 are emitted into the atmosphere every year, most of it in the U.S.

Acid rain is much older on earth than our species itself. And acids have always moved on the land and in the waters from natural causes. But since the industrial revolution humankind, like the sorcerer's apprentice, has turned acid precipitation loose in unprecedented quantities.

Sulfur dioxides and nitrogen oxides, like CO_2, are "fixed" in fossil fuels. When these fuels are burned, these compounds escape into the atmosphere—mainly from smokestacks and industrial plants in the case of sulfur, from vehicle tail pipes in the case of nitrogen. While nature creates sulfur it does not do it in anywhere near such volume as we do. We are now responsible for 90 percent of all the sulfur in circulation in our atmosphere. Even worse, we have so far released less than one-twentieth of the sulfur that it is theoretically possible for us to release. The problem, unless it is resolved, promises to be with us for a long time.

Sulfur dioxide, the leader of this gang of two, has gotten a major boost from us. The total human contribution of this gas in the atmosphere is now over a hundred million tons annually. In the U.S., SO_2 emissions increased by 40 percent between 1950 and the early 1970s, peaking at thirty million tons. In eastern North America, sulfur output from human activities exceeds that from natural sources by a factor of at least ten.

Sulfur dioxide's henchman, NO_x, also owes a great deal to us. The worldwide NO_x emissions from human activities jumped from a little over nine million tons in 1950 to over twenty million tons in the early 1970s and have stayed at that level since.

As the SO_2 and NO_x are turned free in the combustion process, one of two things happens. They either fall very soon as "dry" deposition. Or if they stay aloft long enough—two or three days is enough—they turn to acids and mix with clouds and with rain droplets. At this point they become "wet" deposition. The rain

ionized with these acids is quite literally "acid rain." And after the acids fall to earth in the rain or snow, in the sleet or hail, in the fog or mist, or in the frost or dew, they do their dirty work, mobilizing the heavy metals and attacking life-sustaining nutrients in the soil and life in the waters.

The heavy-duty killing is done by the metals mobilized by the hydrogen ions. These metals, notably aluminum, mercury, and cadmium, begin to move with the chemical and biological processes set in motion, accumulating with time in the soil, in the water, and in living tissue. All of these metals occur naturally in soils and rock, and posed little danger before humans intervened. In the case of perhaps a dozen of these metals, their release into the environment from human activity now far exceeds their release from all natural sources, including soils and volcanoes. The cadmium released by human activity exceeds that released in nature by 20 times, zinc by 23 times, lead by 333 times.

Soil and water are not without their defenses against this invasion. If they have sufficient alkalinity, called "buffering ions," they can throw off the hydrogen ions and their host of metals. Buffering agents in sufficient array prevent the hydrogen ion concentration from rising enough to let acidification set in. But if they do not have sufficient alkalinity, if they are not sufficiently buffered against this onslaught, they gradually fall prey to the invading acids.

Lime is now our main weapon against these unwanted invaders that we ourselves have sent, since it is a strong neutralizer of killer ions. And many lakes and land areas are now limed to protect them from the acids. But liming is only a palliative, not a cure, and an expensive one at that. For a time it raises the pH of the water and the soil, and for a time makes them safe for life, just as a painkiller for a time eases pain in humans. The dangerous aluminum and mercury ions in a lake are temporarily fixed by the lime and sink to the bottom. There, however, they bide their time, concentrate, and go into solution to kill again when the liming stops. But not all the lakes of the world threatened by

acid rain can be continuously limed. It just isn't practical or affordable. It is, at best, a delaying defense, not a final solution.

Acid rain is an adroit commuter. It respects no national or international boundaries. In Europe, chances are the killing acids in one country have come from another country. In Canada the chances are they have come from the U.S. In any state in the U.S., the chances are they have come from another state. At first, when smokestacks were much shorter than they are today, SO_2 tended to stay near the source, creating visibility and health problems locally and falling as dry deposition. So smokestacks were built taller, turning the gases loose over areas far away from the source and, in effect, creating the phenomenon of acid rain.

Tracking acid rain to its source is difficult and often imprecise. There is sharp, sometimes bitter, disagreement over who is responsible, who has or hasn't done enough, and what ought to be done and who ought to do it. Regions are pitted against regions, industries that have said they have done enough are pitted against industries that insist they are in no way responsible. And there are, of course, disagreements among nations. The problem of blame has strained, and continues to strain, relations between the U.S. and Canada, two otherwise close and congenial neighbors. Canada claims that at least half of the acid rain settling on its forests and lakes comes from the U.S. It claims—I believe with justification—that we are moving too slowly against this menace. The acid rain exchange between these two neighbors is not all one-sided. From 10 to 15 percent of the acid rain problem in the northeastern U.S. can be traced back to Canada. Canada recognizes this and is on a program to reduce this unwanted export by 50 percent in the next ten years. The U.S. as yet has no program. All that Canada is asking is that we do what it is doing. We should be willing to do our share. That means committing our nation to a 50 percent reduction in sulfur dioxide emissions within ten years and entering into an agreement with Canada to that effect.

How to pay the bill to stop acid rain is yet another monstrous

problem. It can't be paid by one industry, by one sector, or by one government. It must be a unified effort. Acid rain is by now too widespread, too pervasive, too persistent. How the tab is to be picked up is the job of governments and industries, legislatures and presidents, and states and nations working together. It is a major aspect of the challenge of acid rain.

The Keepers of CO_2

While the greenhouse gases, the CFCs, and the acid rain have been doing their work in the atmosphere, rampant deforestation has spun out of control on the ground.

Its causes spring from a complex mix of demographic, economic, sociological, and political pressures. While technology has played a major part in bringing on the crisis in the atmosphere and the stratosphere, it has had little to do with this other, more earthbound crisis. But like all the other factors, like the gases, the CFCs, and the acid rain, it is leading to the same end—the destruction of our environment.

Behind the headlong bulldozing of the world's great rain forests lies a combination of population pressures, Third World poverty, the inequities of land tenure, pressures to generate foreign exchange for debt payments, and even government subsidies, many of which stimulate destruction of the forests at the public expense. Some environmental groups have linked the loss of forest resources to the type of development strategies pursued by the world's major international banks, which lend to Third World nations.

Randall Hayes, director of the Rainforest Action Network, said in 1987 that international financing of development projects had the direct or indirect effect of destroying tropical rain forests. International financial backing, for instance, is required to launch many of the cattle ranches and agriculture development projects in the rain forests. And these are two of the main reasons the tropical forests are being torched. Hayes argues that if the flow of supporting capital could be stopped, the rate of deforestation

could be slowed. "It's a battle that can be won," he says. "It takes money to finance this destruction. If we can stop the money, we can stop the destruction." The World Bank, one of the major lending institutions that has unwittingly underwritten such destruction, is now one of the trio of organizations that has drafted an action plan to try to reverse the destruction that in part it has fostered.

More land has been cleared for settled cultivation in the past one hundred years than in all the previous centuries of human existence. While the combustion of fossil fuels was pumping 185 billion tons of CO_2 into the atmosphere since 1860, forest clearing was adding another 100 billion tons. Today land conversion, principally deforestation in the tropics, releases an estimated 1.6 billion tons of carbon every year. Forty percent of the carbon escaping into the atmosphere from the rain forests originates in South America, 37 percent in tropical Asia, and 23 percent in tropical Africa. The forests of only five countries—Brazil, Colombia, Indonesia, Ivory Coast, and Thailand—account for half of all carbon emissions. Brazil alone contributes a fifth of the total. Twenty million acres of forest were cleared and burned in the Brazilian Amazon in 1987, releasing 500 million tons of carbon into the atmosphere.

The principal role of the tropical forests in the climate change equation is as harborers of carbon dioxide. Green plants use CO_2 as a fundamental building block of biomass through photosynthesis. When the rain forests were in full and growing array over the earth's equatorial midsection, they were keeping enormous quantities of CO_2 from the atmosphere. All of the earth's trees, shrubs, and soils in consort hold two trillion tons of CO_2— roughly triple the amount stored in the atmosphere. This escapes when vegetation is cleared, burned, or left to decay. Each year this is happening to twenty-eight million acres of rain forest. Eleven million more acres are lost to commercial timber harvests—a total area of trees larger than New York and Vermont combined.

These forests were—and those left are—critical to maintaining

the earth's delicate balance between not enough CO_2 in the atmosphere and too much. The trick to keeping that equilibrium has always been to sequester carbon from the atmosphere in the green plants of the earth and in the oceans. And the great rain forests have been one of the preeminent sequestering grounds. But an area the size of Australia would have to be reforested to store all of the carbon currently released into our atmosphere by our fossil fuel economies. Instead of creating vast new Australia-sized forests, however, we continue to cut down and destroy those we have. And the effort to replace what we destroy lags far behind. Today in the developing countries ten trees are cut down for every one that is replanted. In Africa the ratio is thirty to one. There is an urgent need to replenish this carbon bank before it goes entirely bankrupt.

It is believed that an additional 320 million acres of trees—an area twice the size of Texas—will be needed by the year 2000 to meet the Third World's demand for fuel and industrial wood products and to rehabilitate deteriorating ecosystems.

As with so much that we must now do to steady the planet's reeling systems, we are running out of time. It may already be too little too late to adequately restock the store of the world's keepers of CO_2. With every tick of the clock the Four Horsemen continue to gallop. If we do not act in time to halt deforestation, scale back the rate of warming, get the CFCs out of our lives, and dry up the sources of acid rain, then what are we in for?

5

Where It Is Leading

In Maine, we live with the sea. Between Kittery to the south and Eastport to the northeast we front the Atlantic for thirty-five hundred twisting miles. It is as if one long side of our state, richly indented by bays, estuaries, inlets, and sounds, is a rambling front porch overlooking the water. The ocean is a part of us. It has shaped our character and driven our economy. Through my lifetime it has always been there, limitless and unchanging, as oceans everywhere must have appeared to the human eye through centuries of time. They roll and heave as they have down the ages, lapping the land gently or thundering and pounding at it in their more wrathful moods. Ships of all nations knife through their waters—as ships have done from the days of the great sea captains down to the computerized navies of today.

But beneath that veneer of business-as-usual in the world's great sinks, a time bomb is ticking. The seas hold more than water, life, and ships. They also hold carbon dioxide—the CO_2 from the burning of fossil fuels, which in the atmosphere would be warming the earth. They lap up carbon as sand soaks up water. The capacity of the oceanic reservoir to absorb CO_2 has been estimated at about fifty times that of the atmosphere and twenty

65

times that of the biosphere. As this great volume of CO_2 dissolves out of the air into the surface waters of the sea some of it remains dissolved and is carried to the deeps. Some of it lies at the surface of the water. And some of it crosses the air-sea interface to return to the atmosphere.

Even the seemingly limitless seas can take in only so much CO_2. The biosphere also has its limits, although recent studies indicate that soils and plants of the vast forests of the Northern Hemisphere may be absorbing more CO_2 than once believed, by a process still not clearly understood. The atmosphere must take what CO_2 the seas and the biosphere don't—slightly more than half. However, while locked in the earth's oceans or its biosphere the CO_2 released from burning fossil fuels is not contributing to a warmer world. And to that degree the world's oceans, as the major sink for CO_2, are delaying the coming of the long-predicted, much-feared greenhouse effect.

But they are only delaying it, and even that delay may be ending. We have just experienced the six warmest summers of this century, all in the eighties—1980, 1981, 1983, 1986, 1987, and the torrid summer of 1988. These are harbingers of what will happen in the future as the satiated seas begin to reach their limit for holding carbon dioxide. The climate shift has been very slight so far; the projected warming is only just beginning.

How long do we have before the seas have taken in all the CO_2 they can and the full warming effect of what looks to be a doubling of carbon dioxide levels on the planet by 2030 begins to hit? Scientists speculate that the time lag—the time in which the seas can hold off the worst of the heat—is anywhere from ten to fifty years. Many of us, if the projections hold, will live to experience warming temperatures beyond anything we have yet known.

Godwin Olo Patrick Obasi, a distinguished meteorologist and secretary-general of the World Meteorological Organization, put it this way in an interview with *World Climate Change Report*:

The global warming to which we are already committed is irreversible and will become increasingly evident over the next fifty to one hundred years. . . . Once we pass the level of detectability, the effects of climate change will last despite our efforts to overcome them. A commitment to a two-degree global temperature rise is not noticeable at first because the oceans have been absorbing some of the excess energy, but once the ocean lag is overcome, during the next fifty to one hundred years, we're in for it. By the time we detect it, it will be too late.

Once greenhouse gases get into the atmosphere, they are like the man who came to dinner; they stay. They can hang there for decades or centuries. At current rates they are being released into the atmosphere much faster than they are being removed. Because of this, even if we could hold emissions constant at their present levels they would continue to intensify in the atmosphere for the next century.

This means that even if all emissions of greenhouse gases were halted, those already out will be with us for a long time. It might take as long as several centuries for the oceans to absorb enough carbon to reduce CO_2 to its preindustrial levels.

Precisely how rapidly CO_2 and the other gases and chemicals our activity turns loose into the atmosphere are building up is still a matter of scientific dispute. But it is not unreasonable to expect, if the majority of the scientific community is right, that CO_2 emissions will nearly double from over five billion tons a year in 1985 to over nine billion tons by 2010—by the time a baby born today reaches her twenties. It could triple, even quadruple, by the end of the twenty-first century. As this happens, and as seas reach their capacity to absorb the carbon, the earth is going to warm. It appears inevitable, no matter what we do now to try to stop it. The only question is by how much. Future levels of CO_2 in the atmosphere will depend in part on how drastically we are able to cut future emissions and in part on the capacity of the oceans and the biosphere to absorb them, rather than have them stay airborne. To make a notable difference the

cuts would have to be drastic, far greater than the 20 percent cut recommended by scientists and policymakers as a first step.

If carbon dioxide levels double as foretold, the rise in average global temperature, when it hits full force no later than the middle of the coming century, could be between three degrees and nine degrees Fahrenheit. Scientists generally, with notable exceptions, are now predicting a warming nearer the lower than the upper scale. The increase in temperature will be relatively small at the equator, grow larger toward the higher altitudes, and peak at the poles. If carbon dioxide in the atmosphere triples or quadruples, the warming could soar much higher, to temperatures far beyond the range of human experience.

Sharp fluctuations in temperature are not unique on our planet. Abrupt climatic shifts have often followed shifts in the direction of earth's axis, or jumps in solar luminosity, or sudden injections of CO_2 into the atmosphere, or one-time shots of methane into the environment from geological activity, or changes in the interaction between the oceans and the atmosphere. But these don't compare with what is coming.

What will make the warming of the coming century truly unique will be the enormous velocity with which it is likely to strike. An eight degree Fahrenheit temperature rise, for instance, would equal the entire temperature variation of the last 125,000 years: This gradual increase spread over 125 millennia would be matched within but a single century by the outpouring of greenhouse gases into the atmosphere.

What would such an unprecedented outpouring bring? What is likely to happen? The last change in world temperatures of this magnitude—the gradual warming over many millennia—transformed the landscape of North America, shifting the Atlantic Ocean inland by about a hundred miles, creating the Great Lakes, and changing the composition and location of forests throughout the U.S. Can we expect less this time?

Our Hothouse Future

The telescoping of change of such magnitude into such a short time would bring us a world far different from the one of today. It would be a world none of us would recognize. The landscape would change in ways we can't fully foresee. The earth would have an entirely new contour with an entirely new climate. And when it happens, it would be irreversible.

Here, in kaleidoscopic review, is what could happen with a six degree Fahrenheit rise in temperature:

The earth's present climate zones and storm tracks would shift dramatically northward, driving millions of displaced people, plants, and animals with them. Thermal swelling within the seas and water from melting landborne glaciers could raise sea levels by three feet, wiping out rice fields in Asia, destroying precious coastal wetlands worldwide, drowning Venice, Cairo, Shanghai, and the Florida Keys, and threatening shorelines along every ocean side. It would cost the cities along the ocean's edge on the east coast of North America alone in the magnitude of $100 billion to hold back the threatening Atlantic. It would cost Charleston, South Carolina, protected today only by the Battery, its six-foot-high seawall and promenade, $1.5 billion to save itself from the rising sea. If nothing is done to prevent it, half of that historic city would be permanently flooded. The Netherlands, which has traditionally spent more to hold the ocean at bay behind its 250 miles of dikes and 120 miles of sand dunes than it has spent on defense, would have to take extreme measures to avoid going under—at a cost of another $10 billion. The 1,196 low-lying islands of the Maldives, only six feet above sea level at their highest point, could be swamped by a sudden storm surge with catastrophic, perhaps fatal results. The Arctic Sea could become navigable, raising profound security implications. Dramatic northward shifts in rainfall would turn the now fertile midlatitudes of the world—the breadbasket of the American midwest—into rangeland at best, a dust bowl at worst. As much

as half of the farm acreage in the southeastern United States might be lost. Monsoon patterns would shift, throwing agriculture in Asia into chaos. Ocean currents would veer to new courses, wiping out whole fisheries.

Climatic extremes would trigger meteorological chaos—raging hurricanes such as we have never seen, capable of killing millions of people; uncommonly long, record-breaking heat waves; and profound drought that could drive Africa and the entire Indian subcontinent over the edge into mass starvation. By the time today's teenagers are ready to retire, the District of Columbia would be having twelve days a year of one hundred degree temperatures and higher; it has only one a year now. Eighty-seven days of the year would see temperatures of ninety degrees or more in the nation's capital; there are only thirty-six now. Days of 122-degree heat, such as Phoenix, Arizona experienced in the summer of 1990, could become commonplace, rather than unprecedented, in the American Southwest. Siberia and the Yukon could become the choice places on earth to live.

What such ever-rising temperatures and continued warming through a century to three centuries might bring is almost incomprehensible. A large, sustained, ever-increasing warming of earth over that long a time could melt the ice caps covering Greenland and disintegrate the West Antarctic ice sheet. The rise in sea level at that point is impossible to predict and terrible to contemplate. But it could be as high as twenty feet or more. A rise of fifteen feet would put major parts of San Francisco, New Orleans, Boston, Miami, New York, and most of the rest of the U.S. coastline under water.

The prospect for the planet under the higher temperatures and rising sea levels now predicted within our own lifetimes is so-bering enough. The world of Eric and Luisa could become our world before we die. We are on the brink of it even now. Even if we could stop all greenhouse gas emissions today, we would still be committed to a temperature increase worldwide of two to four degrees Fahrenheit by the middle of the twenty-first cen-

tury. It would be warmer then than it has been for the past two million years. Unchecked it would match nuclear war in its potential for devastation.

The human displacement could be catastrophic, with the prospect of a thronging of tens of millions of environmental refugees over the earth as more and more areas of the planet become unfit for human habitation. A new wave of migration triggered for a whole new reason—an ongoing environmental crisis—now looms. We had a small taste of it in the U.S. in the Dust Bowl of the 1930s. The Joads from John Steinbeck's *The Grapes of Wrath* were environmental refugees. What happened then in Oklahoma is already happening in many other parts of the earth. It can only worsen in a warming world.

Desertification, closely related to the natural disaster that displaced the Joads, is now the environmental anomaly driving most of today's environmental refugees from their homelands. An array of dislocating catastrophes such as earthquakes, floods, cyclones, avalanches, mudslides, and toxic spills and radioactive accidents is the second major cause. In the face of these and the invading sand, environmental refugees have now become the single largest class of displaced persons in the world. They are driven out for one of three causes. Either they have been displaced only temporarily because of local one-time disruptions, such as an avalanche or an earthquake or a flood. Or the environmental degradation has undermined their livelihood or threatened their health and forced them out. Or desertification or some other permanent change has driven them out for good. This last cause is the largest and the fastest growing of them all. Some of the permanently displaced roam from place to place, from one plot of marginal land to another and yet another, using up the land and making still more desert. Others, in growing numbers, simply throng to the cities.

Tomorrow's preeminent maker of environmental refugees will probably be a rising sea. It is likely to displace, perhaps dwarf, desertification as the leading cause of homelessness. Sir Crispin

Tickell, the United Kingdom's Representative to the United Nations, has pictured what might happen. In an address in London on June 5, 1989, he said:

> A heavy concentration of people is at present in low-lying coastal areas or along the world's great river systems. Nearly one-third of humanity lives within sixty kilometers of a coastline. A rise in median sea level of only twenty-five centimeters [less than a foot] would have substantial effects. The industrial countries might be able to construct new sea defenses to protect vulnerable areas, but even they would have vulnerability in coping with high tides and storm surges of a kind which might be more common. For most poor countries such defenses would be out of the question. Many of those living and working in for example the delta areas of the Nile, the Ganges, and the Yangtze would be forced out of their homes and livelihood. Some islands such as the Maldives in the Indian Ocean and Kiribati, Tuvalu, and the Marshall Islands in the Pacific would become uninhabitable. Bangladesh with its population of over one hundred million and Egypt with its population of around seventy million would be particularly affected. A further rise in sea levels—up to half a meter and beyond—would have more drastic results. The world would look a different place.

A rising sea, caused mainly by thermal expansion of ocean waters, is a certain and far-reaching consequence of a warming world. Yet it is a consequence we have not planned for. As William D. Ruckelshaus, a former EPA administrator, has written, "We have planned our cities, developed our manufacturing techniques, and chosen our environmental protection strategies on the assumption of a stable sea level."

By the best estimate, a three-foot rise in sea level (a possibility, although a one- to two-foot rise is now more commonly predicted in a doubling of carbon dioxide in the atmosphere) would drown 25 to 80 percent of the present U.S. coastal wetlands. Unless we change our assumption of a stable sea level, from five thousand to ten thousand square miles of dry land could go under in the

U.S. sometime in the next century. Without any effort to hold back the sea, most of the nineteen-thousand-mile U.S. shoreline one hundred feet from the water's edge would go under, even in the most conservative estimates. About 70 percent of the land loss would be in the Southeast, especially in Florida, Louisiana, and North Carolina. The Gulf of Mexico could surge inland into Louisiana as far as thirty miles. The eastern shore of the Chesapeake and the Delaware bays would also be hard hit. The Southeast is rich in wetlands and shore-hugging sea life. Over 85 percent of the nation's wetlands are there, 40 percent of them in Louisiana. Over 40 percent of the nation's finfish and 70 percent of its shellfish are harvested in the region.

Wetlands are not fixed in space and time. Like all living things, they can migrate—if they are not blocked, as they well might be as we scramble to protect developed shorelines from the sea. Even if not blocked, a third to two-thirds of every wetland acre in the country could be lost. If they are prevented from migrating out of harm's way by our protection of developed stretches of the coastline, the loss could be as high as eight acres out of every ten by 2030.

Twelve of the country's twenty biggest cities lie on tidal waterfronts—Baltimore, Boston, Houston, Los Angeles, Miami, New York, Philadelphia-Wilmington, San Francisco–Oakland, San Diego, Seattle, Tampa–St. Petersburg, and Washington, D.C. The cost of protecting these cities and the less populated stretches of developed shoreline from the encroaching sea would be enormous. Experts have put the price tag at $73 billion to $111 billion (in 1985 dollars) by 2100. This would pay for building bulkheads and levees, pumping sand, and raising barrier islands. It could cost as much as $50 billion to $75 billion to elevate beaches, houses, lands, and roadways on developed barrier islands. Even with these outlays an estimated seven thousand acres of dry land, an area the size of Massachusetts, could not be saved.

Miami and Charleston are two striking examples of vulnera-

bility to a rising sea. Miami exists and grows and prospers on what engineers call a "hydrologic masterwork" of natural and artificial systems that hold back both the swamp and the sea. A three-foot rise in sea level would drive the city to extreme measures to survive. It would have to build a costly system of seawalls and dikes, and even that might not save it. The elaborate system of pumps and drainage that now maintains the integrity of Miami's highly porous aquifer could be overwhelmed. Then roads would buckle, bridge abutments would sink, and much of Miami's land area would be reclaimed by the swamp.

How Charleston would have to spend its $1.5 billion to save itself illustrates what many other cities, large and small, would be in for. According to Charleston mayor Joseph P. Riley, who says "mayors' jobs are pragmatic ones, we see government at the sidewalk level," all of those sidewalks in his city would have to be raised and rebuilt. He says a three- to five-foot rise in sea level over the next one hundred years would inundate a substantial part of the city. Besides the sidewalks, the streets and most of the rest of the basic infrastructure of the city would have to be rebuilt. Seawalls fronting the bay would have to be raised. Pump stations would have to be built to pump the city's warm water surge out against the tide, because most of its outfalls are now below mean high water. Such things are costly. Buildings would have to be modified wholesale. All of the city's hospitals have their emergency generating plants on the first floor. They would have to be raised. All the bridges over the water are now built for ships to clear at current sea levels; they would have to be rebuilt. The low-lying causeways, the city's access to its sea islands, would have to be restructured. Old landfills, built with no thought of a rising sea, would have to be either removed or protected from the infiltrating water, or a Pandora's box of pollution would be opened up anew on the city.

Around the world cities such as Venice, Bangkok, and Taipei would be inundated. In some parts of the world subsidence would make league with the rising seas to intensify the problem. Bang-

ladesh, a land of natural calamities, is already subsiding. A sea rising one to three feet to meet the sinking land could put 16 to 28 percent of that nation, which is little more than a mosaic of rivers on a flat and vulnerable delta, under water. Bangladesh as it is known today would virtually cease to exist. There is no higher ground for its people to move to; thirty-eight million of them could become environmental refugees.

As much as 15 percent of Egypt's teeming Nile delta could go under in a similar rising of the sea. Such a rise would inundate vast areas of the East China coastal plain, including Shanghai, China's largest port and most populated city. The Tai Hu Lake and surrounding lakes would become part of the East China Sea. Congming Island, the third largest in China, would disappear. In the face of such a rise in sea level China would have to build Netherlands-style dikes, move coastal residents inland, reorganize and rebuild its coastal industries, and relocate and replan its ocean-fronting cities and towns.

The rising temperatures could set in motion a series of extreme and catastrophic climatic events. Heat waves, unbearable for some human beings in their intensity, would be virtually certain. The first of the hottest summers of this decade, the summer of 1980, brought us a preview. St. Louis suffered through sixteen days of above one-hundred-degree temperatures. Dallas had forty-two consecutive days over one hundred degrees. The death toll nationally from the heat that year was several times above normal. Major heat waves of the past have been devastating. More than 9,000 people died in the Midwest in a blazing heat wave in 1901. Nearly 5,000 died nationwide in the searing summer of 1936. Without preparations for offsetting it, a doubled CO_2 level in the coming century could raise summertime deaths in the U.S. from the current 1,156 a year to over 7,000 by one projection. The elderly—seniors above sixty-five—would be particularly vulnerable, accounting for 70 percent of those deaths.

Rapidly changing temperatures could stir out of the sea hurricanes unprecedented in history for violence, strength, and ca-

pacity to destroy. Hurricanes require ocean temperatures of eighty degrees or warmer. Global warming on a magnitude now predicted would not only permit more of them to form in the warm waters where they have always formed, but would allow them to build at higher latitudes as well, and extend their season on both ends of the summer. The deadliest hurricane on record battered Bangladesh in 1970, killing three hundred thousand people. The most damaging hurricane ever to hit the U.S. raked Galveston in 1900, killing six thousand—the worst natural disaster in U.S. history. Neither of these matched in force and power the hurricanes that could be expected in a dramatically warming world of the twenty-first century.

Two pioneers in the study of atmospheric chemistry, Thomas E. Graedel of Bell Laboratories and Paul J. Crutzen of the Max Planck Institute for Chemistry in Mainz, West Germany, writing in *Scientific American,* put the possibilities this way:

> What is particularly troubling is the possibility of unwelcome surprises, as human activities continue to tax an atmosphere whose inner workings and interactions with organisms and nonliving materials are incompletely understood. The Antarctic ozone hole is a particularly ominous example of the surprises that may be lurking ahead. Its unexpected severity has demonstrated beyond doubt that the atmosphere can be exquisitely sensitive to what seem to be small chemical perturbations and that the manifestations of such perturbations can arise much faster than even the most astute scientists could expect.

The terrifying pace of climate change in the next century could exceed by many times the ability of trees and vegetation, and some animal species, to survive it or migrate to cooler climates. Extinction would be inevitable for many. In less than a century several hundred million years of evolution of earth's flora and fauna could be undone. Gone in a warming world would be the polar bear's habitat if the Arctic ice sheet melts. Gone would be the Florida panther if the rising sea inundates its habitat. Gone would be the waterfowl populations along the midcontinent fly-

way in North America if the prairie potholes in the upper Midwest dry up permanently.

Harvard's Edward O. Wilson, one of the first to ring the alarm on the global decline in biological diversity and to spell out its consequences, says in *Scientific American*:

> The world biota is trapped as though in a vise. On one side it is being swiftly reduced by deforestation. On the other it is threatened by climatic warming brought on by the greenhouse effect. Whereas habitat loss is most destructive to tropical biotas, climatic warming is expected to have a greater impact on the biotas of the cold temperate regions and polar regions. A poleward shift of climate at the rate of one hundred kilometers or more per century, which is considered at least a possibility, would leave wildlife preserves and entire species ranges behind, and many kinds of plants and animals could not migrate fast enough to keep up.

Extinction of species has always been with us. It is the way of life on the planet. Of all the species that have existed since the emergence of life 3.6 billion years ago, at least 90 percent have disappeared. Yet the rate of extinction of the past does not remotely compare with what we are in for in the warming world to come. The average rate of natural extinction has moved in very slow motion through the ages. It has ranged, without human intervention, from 2 to 4.6 families of species per million years, rising to an average 19.3 families per million years during the five prehistoric episodes of mass extinctions. In the next one hundred years alone we may see the unprecedented extinction of 50 families of plants—a quarter of all plant families on earth—together with many associated animal families and insects. Species in the earth's tropical forest are particularly vulnerable to what may be coming. Many delicate and specialized species in the dense, wet rain forests are incapable of surviving even a moderate disruption of their habitats. They can't even survive the depredations of human activity. They could not hope to survive a cataclysmic climate change.

The rising temperatures and the rising seas between them could

wipe out entire fragile oceanic coral reef systems that are nearly as rich in their diversity of life as the rain forests. A shift in the course of the Gulf Stream, a possibility in a warming world, could, ironically, leave many species of marine life behind in waters too cold for survival. Changes in upwelling zones could sweep other marine species long accustomed to stable environments into oblivion. Moreover, all of these changes in the sea would take place in ecosystems that ecologist Norman Myers says "are beyond helping hands." James Titus, a sea-level specialist at the Environmental Protection Agency, predicts that "we'll be mere spectators in the adjustments to climate change [in the oceans]. People will have to adapt to whatever the fish decide to do."

For those species rooted to the earth, the toll could be particularly high and the changes over time dramatic. Over the thousands of years since the last ice age there has been a warming commensurate with what is now likely to occur in the coming century. But those temperatures rose slowly enough for the forests in the temperate zones to migrate with the change. The temperatures in the coming warming would unreasonably telescope the escape window, causing forest migrations—or diebacks —unheard of in history. It is believed that climate change on the order often predicted could move the southern boundary of the eastern hemlock, yellow birch, beech, and sugar maple range in North America four hundred miles northward. The southern pine forests could shift three hundred miles northward into the present hardwood forests of eastern Pennsylvania and New Jersey. A mass dieback of forests in the Southeast is possible. Historically, forests migrate at placid rates—on the order of six to thirty miles a century. By way of contrast, cattle egrets, which migrate on wings, can colonize an entire continent within forty years. But all too often the fastest animals can only migrate as fast as the slowest plant or animal—if those plants and animals are its main source of food.

To survive the coming earth warming many trees would have

to move ten times faster than in any past migration. And in the coming flight for their lives, species will no longer have a free and clear path to safety, their way impeded only by natural barriers. Human beings, who will have triggered this mass migration, are also now blocking the way with their farmlands, highways, and cities. To a migrating forest, a city is virtually unpassable. "Few animals or plants," Robert Peters of the World Wildlife Fund has said, "would be able to cross Los Angeles on the way to the promised land."

The dieback of forests would start to become noticeable after a rise in temperature of 1.5 degrees, then come with a rush. The dieback could start in thirty years and be virtually completed within sixty to eighty years. All the while these forests, unless we can help them, will be hit not only by warming, but by acid rain, and by bombardment from ultraviolet rays penetrating through the shredded ozone layer. Drier soils on the ground could trigger more frequent forest fires. Warmer temperatures could set a host of migrating pests on forests that have up to now been out of their reach. Pathogens and changes in oxidant formation could sap what resilience many of these trees have left.

As for the great rain forests of the tropical world, they could become virtually extinct by the end of this century, if the present pace of their destruction holds. We face the possibility that there could be little virgin forest left outside of the Zaire Basin, the western half of the Brazilian Amazon, the Guyana tract in northern South America, and parts of the island of New Guinea. And their days would be numbered as well, as further world demand for their products continues to quicken and the number of farms and fields and roads hewed out of the forests continues to multiply.

Recent computer models devised by Jagadish Shukla and Piers Sellers of the University of Maryland Center for Ocean-Land Atmosphere Interactions and Carlos Nobre of the Brazilian Space Research Institute suggest that if the rain forests become grassland within the next century—a distinct possibility—the impact

on the weather worldwide could be dramatic. Rainfall in the Amazon could drop from an average one hundred inches a year to seventy-five inches. Average temperatures in the region would climb by nearly five degrees Fahrenheit. The dry season would lengthen. The chances of the forest ever returning would be slim. And world temperatures might be affected in ways we cannot now predict.

If crops, like trees, must shift northward from the farm-rich American Midwest to escape the rising heat, they could come onto soils in Minnesota, Wisconsin, and Michigan more nutrient-poor than the soils they are accustomed to in the Corn Belt. Fleeing crops would also find a more barren welcome in Scandinavia and in Canada. It would take centuries for more productive soils to form in these more northern regions.

Parts of the world that are water-short today, such as the American West, would be even more so in a warmer world. Warmer temperatures would increase the proportion of rain to snow, cause earlier runoff of winter snowpacks, heighten evaporation, and diminish further the available water supply. A temperature rise of 3.6 degrees Fahrenheit, now seen as inevitable, and a 10 percent drop in precipitation could cut water supplies in each of the seven western river basins by nearly half to three-quarters. The Rio Grande Basin could come up short by 76 percent; the Missouri, 64 percent; the Arkansas-White-Red, 54 percent; the Texas Gulf, 50 percent; the Upper Colorado, 40 percent; the Lower Colorado, 57 percent; and California, 44 percent. The average supply over all seven of these great water resource regions would be cut in half. One need not tell a rancher in the water-short West what this would mean and the harm it would do.

The higher temperatures would aggravate air pollution conditions over many cities. A temperature rise of seven degrees in the San Francisco Bay area would raise ozone pollution levels by 20 percent. While dealing with the problem of rising pollution in the air above, the world's most heavily populated ocean-front-

ing cities would have to deal on the ground simultaneously with intruding salt water from a rising sea. It is estimated that the coming climate change could cost cities in the New York–Philadelphia corridor $3 billion to $7 billion in capital construction.

In a warmer world, demand for electricity by the year 2040 could be three times what it was in 1980. Chauncey Starr, president emeritus and director of the Electric Power Research Institute, believes that by the year 2060 electricity generation may eat up as much primary energy as the world consumes in total today. This does not hold a lot of promise for a dramatic cutback in fossil-fuel consumption. That energy source looks to be with us a long time, or until alternative renewable sources of energy are developed in enough quantity to take up the slack.

The annual cost for meeting this surge in demand for electricity would be between $33 billion and $73 billion (in 1986 dollars) in the U.S. alone. The cumulative cost of more power-plant capacity could soar to between $175 billion and $325 billion. Demands on the electric utilities, one of the chief contributors to global climate change, could be financially devastating. Even a one-degree rise in temperature could be disastrous if the utilities read it wrong. One New York utility has estimated it could lose $11 million if it planned for a one-degree temperature rise that never happened, but $55 million if it didn't plan for it and it happened by 2015.

The Environmental Protection Agency has considered in detail the potential impact of global climate change on four major areas of the U.S.: California, the Southeast, the Great Lakes, and the Great Plains. Here are thumbnail sketches of what may happen in each of these regions as the earth warms:

California. Annual deliveries of water from water-rich northern California to water-short southern California over the State Water Project would drop 7 to 16 percent because of lighter snowpack and earlier runoff. Water quality would fall sharply in the state's subalpine lakes. The rising sea levels on the coast would

increase salinity in San Francisco Bay, cause a shift from fresh-water to saltwater species, inundate wetlands, and alter waterfowl habitats. In the rich agricultural Central Valley the demand for irrigation would intensify, groundwater levels would drop, water quality would fall, and crop production would be affected in ways now hard to predict. Demand for electricity would jump and smog would increase.

Southeast. The amount of cultivated acreage would fall. Corn and soybean yields would diminish. Forests would die back sharply over thirty to eighty years, converting to grassland. Agricultural pests would multiply. There would be mass inundations of the region's rich wetlands. Dry land would submerge under rising waters. Fish and shellfish populations would shrink.

Great Lakes. Lake levels could fall by as much as eight feet. The duration of the ice cover on the lakes could shorten by one to three months. New dredging of harbors and channels might become necessary. Fish habitats are likely to increase in the fall, winter, and spring and decrease in the summer. Some species would grow in numbers, new species would possibly invade the lakes. The region's rich forests would shift from mixed northern hardwood and oak to oak savannas and grassland. Mixed northern hardwood and boreal forests would change to all northern hardwood. There would be a dramatic shift of crops northward.

Great Plains. Crop yields in this region, the breadbasket of the world, could decline by 4 to 22 percent. Demand would quicken for irrigation as the land became drier. As in all the other regions, water quality would decline and demand for electricity would increase.

Global warming alone does not give a complete picture of the changes that will come with a rapidly changing climate. It is but one of the Four Horsemen threatening us. There are three other

members of this grim gang at work on our planet, in our atmosphere, and in our stratosphere.

The CFCs now in the ozone layer or on their way there are bound to further shred the planet's ultraviolet shield, with alarming consequences. Assuming a modest 3 percent per year increase in CFC emissions, a tenth of the ozone layer could be depleted by the mid-twenty-first century. This amount of destruction to the earth's only shield against the sun's lethal rays would be a biological disaster. A 5 to 20 percent jump in the amount of unblocked radiation bombarding earth through rifts in the ozone layer could cause skin cancer in millions of people who might otherwise never have it. Ozone depletion on that magnitude could trigger 3 million to 15 million new cases of basal squamous cell carcinoma, a relatively mild form of skin cancer despite its formidable name, just in Americans born before 2075. Some 52,000 to 252,000 people would die from it. The rays would also bring with them a more lethal form of skin cancer—melanoma—to 31,000 to 126,000 Americans born before 2075, killing 7,000 to 30,000 of them. Melanoma incidence, and deaths from it, is already on the rise among Caucasian populations around the world (other ethnic groups are rarely affected by these two kinds of skin cancer). Melanoma deaths are up fivefold over the past fifty years in Australia, up 83 percent over the past seven years in the U.S., and increasing 3 to 7 percent a year worldwide.

Dermatologists who specialize in these forms of cancer say there is now no question that virtually all nonmelanoma skin cancers are caused by chronic exposure to ultraviolet radiation. "The relationship is such," says Dr. Fred Urbach of the Skin and Cancer Hospital at Temple University, "that if everybody lived 250 years, everybody would get skin cancer. The reason why some of us do not is because we have somewhat less exposure and we have a competing risk; we die before we get old enough to develop skin cancer." For many, perhaps millions, wide holes in the ozone layer that let in higher-than-normal levels of ultraviolet light would drastically shorten those odds.

More ultraviolet rays beaming down from the sun through the rifts in the ozone could also quicken the incidence of cataracts by half a million, to nearly three million, striking people earlier in life—and not just Caucasians. This menacing ultraviolet light, unabsorbed by a shredded ozone layer, would also depress the human immune system in ways that are not yet entirely clear, reduce crop yields, disrupt the chain of marine life in the seas, and render plastics brittle and breakable.

It would affect all life in some way, and none perhaps more disastrously than the plant life both in the sea and on the land. Very little ultraviolet radiation is needed to "cook" sensitive phytoplankton floating near the surface of the oceans. Phytoplankton are the grass of the sea, the microscopic floating plants that are the basic building blocks of the aquatic life chain. Ultraviolet light stunts photosynthesis in phytoplankton, and sharply enhanced ultraviolet light could change their pigmentation and cause a shift in its species composition. Particularly vulnerable are the species of phytoplankton that are most sensitive—the nanoplankton and the picoplankton—on which krill and other small marine organisms feed. Since these small organisms and krill are the basic food of larger marine animals, including fish and whales, the repercussions would be felt all the way up the life chain.

For photobiologists, those specialists who worry about the effects of the sun's light on plants, fungi, crabs, and worms on earth, depletion of the ozone layer is a nightmare. In a meeting of the American Society for Photobiology in Colorado Springs in 1988, their president-elect, Thomas Coohill, said: "Any depletion in the ozone layer means the genetic material starts absorbing more ultraviolet light, and it changes it. For evolution to occur, the genetic material has to be stable. Organisms don't have enough time to catch up from an evolutionary point of view."

And this leads to trouble everywhere. "Things like plankton," Coohill said, "seem to be at a level where a small change can

have drastic effects. If this [change] occurs on a large scale the effects reverberate throughout the food chain. . . . It would be a subtle change. You wouldn't see crops dying in the field. It's an innocuous thing and the next thing you know, people are starving. In America we don't worry so much about starvation. We worry mostly about the increased skin cancer. But when you look at it on a global scale you have to say that more important than skin cancer are the effects on plant life and animal life."

Much has been written, in this book and elsewhere, about the potential threat to human survival posed by depletion of the ozone layer. Not enough attention has been paid to the one place on earth where large-scale depletion is a reality: Antarctica—the frozen continent, and one of the richest habitats in the world of the plankton that so concern Dr. Coohill.

Two hundred million years ago what is now Antarctica was part of a large supercontinent known as Gonwanaland. It included what are now the continents of Antarctica, Africa, Australia, and South America, as well as that part of Asia that is now India. About 160 million years ago Gonwanaland broke apart and its components gradually drifted to their current locations. Thus was Antarctica created, five and a half million square miles of uninhabitable land covered by an ice sheet nearly one and a half miles thick.

It was above this austere land that CFCs released around the world gathered and began to destroy the ozone layer. In a sense we have been fortunate. Had it occurred over a heavily populated continent, the first evidence might have been a dramatic increase in human skin cancers. That has not happened because only a few thousand people—mostly researchers and construction and maintenance workers—are present on Antarctica at any given time, and few if any of them will spend their lifetimes there.

Nonetheless there will likely be other adverse effects in the region. The most serious could be a failure of the food system upon which those animals which inhabit the region depend—

beginning with the plankton. In *Time* magazine in early 1990 Michael D. Lemonick reported:

> Marine ecologist Sayed El-Sayed of Texas A&M University discovered two years ago at Palmer Station, a U.S. base on the Antarctic Peninsula, that high levels of ultraviolet damage the chlorophyll pigment vital for photosynthesis in phytoplankton, slowing the marine plants' growth rate by as much as 30 percent. That, in turn, could threaten krill, shrimplike creatures that feed on phytoplankton and are a key link in Antarctica's food chain. Says El-Sayed: "Fish, whales, penguins, and winged birds all depend very heavily on krill. If anything happened to the krill population, the whole system would collapse."

Such a collapse would, of course, be devastating to the affected species. For their sakes, as well as ours, we must mend the hole in the sky and protect Antarctica from the kind of environmental assaults that have so profoundly altered the world's other continents. As Soviet President Mikhail Gorbachev has said, in pledging his country's resources to preventing such environmental assaults on the Antarctic, "Our grandchildren will never forgive us if we fail to preserve this phenomenal ecological system."

Another assault that may have little direct effect on the Antarctic continues, however, to threaten the environment elsewhere. And it is measured in multitudes.

6

The Fifth Horseman

A steady and rising drumbeat accompanies the gathering environmental tragedy. And it is mounting toward a crescendo that ultimately threatens to drown out everything. This pounding counterpoint is population growth in the Third World. Like Ravel's "Bolero," it rises steadily in intensity, thundering ever upward in pitch, becoming ever more pervasive. Headlong growth in human numbers has become in effect a Fifth Horseman, a terrifying cohort to the four despoilers of the world environment.

It took nearly seventeen hundred years for the world population to double for the first time in recorded history. It has doubled three times since then. The next doubling, from the present 5 billion to more than 9 billion, will take less than half a century. The farther back in history one looks, the more unreliable the count becomes. But we can extrapolate. In 2 million B.C. there were perhaps 100,000 food-gathering bipeds on earth, the most distant of our ancestors. By the beginning of settled agriculture, about 8000 B.C., the world's population had probably reached 5 million. At the time of Christ's birth it had passed 200 million, less than the size of the U.S. population today,

probably half of that number living in China. By A.D. 1650 world population had expanded to 500 million. Then the population bomb detonated. By 1750 there were 1 billion, 2 billion by 1900, 4.4 billion by 1980, more than 5 billion today.

Already in this century the population of the planet has more than lapped itself. Within the next forty years our human world of 5 billion must make room in a finite environment for yet another entire human world of like size. Each year the world adds the population equivalent of a good-sized Third World nation—a Mexico for instance, some 80 million people. We are approaching the time, not many generations from now, when the carrying capacity of earth will simply be exceeded if population growth is not checked.

The population explosion is keeping dismal pace with the growth of carbon dioxide itself. Nine of every ten people in that new human world that will be added within the next half century will be born in the Third World. The total population of the planet will be younger than today, more urban, and poor.

Here is the prospect for parts of the Third World in forty years, unless something is done to bring down fertility rates: India, overburdened even now by the crushing weight of over-population, will double in human numbers by 2030. To its population of 800 million will be added another billion, making it 40 percent larger than China today. Bangladesh, that environmentally ill-starred nation clinging to a flood-ridden river delta, will nearly triple in population. From its present 104 million it will grow to 342 million, all of them crammed into a space the size of Wisconsin, on a flatland battered alternately by flood and drought. Ethiopia's 46 million will swell by four times. Nigeria, just over 100 million today, will more than quadruple to 529 million. Mexico will double in size from its more than 80 million. Kenya's 17 million, far too many already for its sparse supply of arable land, will have quintupled by the end of the four decades. The total population in the Third World in 1980 was 3.3 billion. It will be at 7 billion by 2025 and over 8.5 billion by 2050.

Africa's population will be 2.3 billion, a tenfold increase over a century's time. All of this will happen if something isn't done to stem the tide.

Most of the developing nations recognize the consequences of such multiplication of their numbers. In the early 1980s, fifty-five Third World governments declared that population growth in their countries threatens to strangle their economic growth. The heads of state of more than half of the Third World countries have signed a statement to the United Nations that says, in part: "If this unprecedented population growth continues, future generations of children will not have adequate food, housing, medical care, education, natural resources, and employment opportunities." The heads of government of China, India, Bangladesh, Thailand, Indonesia, Egypt, Morocco, Kenya, and Nigeria all signed. These nations do not always share common interests. But they share this common threat.

Ever more people burn ever more fossil fuels, causing ever more pollution. And they cut and burn ever more rain forests, their chief resource, so that they can exist. The ramifications of unbridled continued population growth are self-evident. The new billions will accelerate all the harmful forces afoot in our environment today and bring unendurable pressure to bear on the world's finite natural resources. They will inject yet another unknown into the already difficult art of predicting the true extent of future earth warming. Clearly the continued multiplication of human numbers in the Third World, coupled with the drive to sustain economic development there, is an explosive mixture. In the absence of major technological breakthroughs, it will set off yet another escalation of greenhouse gases into the atmosphere. Eventually the carrying capacity of the planet could simply be exceeded, rendering the the earth virtually unlivable. No nation and no people, rich or poor, north or south, will be exempt from the consequences.

There is a troubling twist to this population anaconda that threatens to strangle us. The population is not only exploding,

it is increasingly concentrating in the urban centers of the world. Not only will 90 percent of those born in the coming human flood be from the Third World, they will be city dwellers—and in cities unable even now to keep pace with their numbers. The numbers are overwhelming: In just forty years, since 1950, the number of people living in cities worldwide has nearly tripled, increasing by one and a quarter billion. In the sixty years between 1920 and 1980, the rush of people to the cities of the Third World was particularly breathtaking: The population of Third World cities increased tenfold, from a hundred million to a billion. By the turn of the century another three-quarter billion people will live in those cities.

We are clearly experiencing an urban revolution. Moreover, it is a revolution that is no longer taking place in the New Yorks or the San Franciscos or the Londons of the world. It is taking place in Nairobi, Dar es Salaam, Nouakchott, Lusaka, Kinshasa, Seoul, Baghdad, Dakar, Amman, Bombay, Jakarta, Mexico City, Manila, São Paulo, Bogotá, and Managua. That is where most of the Third World population will be living fifty years from now, in cities already stressed by too many people and least able give the millions pouring into them anything approaching decent services, a roof over their heads, or jobs. The enormous pressures for shelter and services for this overwhelming flood of refugees is already overtaxing Third World cities. Housing is dilapidated at best, nonexistent at worst. Civic buildings are in disrepair and decay. Public transportation is inadequate. Roads are underdeveloped. Public facilities are overused. In all too many Third World cities, the water supply is contaminated by sewage. Diseases are rampant—acute respiratory ailments, tuberculosis, and internal parasites. Diarrhea, dysentery, hepatitis, and typhoid fever—the dread diseases of poor sanitation and contaminated drinking water—are endemic. And the dying are the young. In the slums of many cities in the developing countries, poor parents can expect to see one in four of their children die of serious malnutrition before they reach the age of five.

Cities of the industrial world have their own very real and serious problems—deteriorating infrastructures, inner-city decay, environmental disintegration, ghetto minorities, and the poor trapped in a downward spiral of ever more poverty. But their problems don't begin to compare with the problems of the burgeoning Third World cities. Moreover, industrial nation cities have the means and resources to deal with their problems. Most Third World cities don't.

The World Commission on Environment and Development, in *Our Common Future*, its landmark report of 1987, paints this bleak picture:

Out of India's 3,119 towns and cities, only 209 had partial and only 8 had full sewage and sewage treatment facilities. On the river Ganges, 114 cities each with fifty thousand or more inhabitants dump untreated sewage into the river every day. DDT factories, tanneries, paper and pulp mills, petrochemical and fertilizer complexes, rubber factories, and a host of others use the river to get rid of their wastes. The Hooghly estuary (near Calcutta) is choked with untreated industrial wastes from more than 150 major factories around Calcutta. Sixty percent of Calcutta's population suffer from pneumonia, bronchitis, and other respiratory diseases related to air pollution.

Chinese industries, most of which use coal in outdated furnaces and boilers, are concentrated around 20 cities and ensure a high level of air pollution. Lung cancer mortality in Chinese cities is four to seven times higher than in the nation as a whole, and the difference is largely attributable to heavy air pollution.

In Malaysia, the highly urbanized Klang Valley (which includes the capital, Kuala Lumpur) has two to three times the pollution levels of major cities in the United States, and the Klang river system is heavily contaminated with agricultural and industrial effluents and sewage.

Jorge Hardoy, of the International Institute for Environment and Development, told the commission in a public hearing in São Paulo in 1985: "Given the distribution of incomes, given

the foreseeable availability of resources—national, local, and worldwide—given present technology, and given the present weakness of local government and the lack of interest of national governments in resettlement problems, I don't see any hope for the Third World city."

The flip side of the undeveloped world's birth problem is its death problem. The high mortality rates are as disturbing as the high birth rates. Again it is the young, the Luisas of the Third World, who are dying. In Ghana, Africa's richest country, 50 percent of the children never reach the age of fifteen. The majority of those who do never reach thirty-five. In the developing world generally children under five account for 20 percent of the population but for more than 60 percent of the deaths.

It has been suggested that to stabilize world population three things—poverty, fertility, and mortality—must be lowered and one thing raised: the status of women. It may be possible to halt world population at about eight billion by the middle of the twenty-first century if these four things are done. Whatever raises the status of women economically and socially lowers fertility rates. It's a given. Poverty, on the other hand, invariably raises both fertility and mortality rates.

Two prominent nations with teeming numbers have shown that fertility rates can be lowered. Both Japan and China have made dramatic moves to hold their populations in check in this half of the twentieth century. And both have in effect cut their rates of population growth in half in a matter of years. After World War II, Japan suddenly found itself forced to live largely on resources within its own borders. The nation could not bear to have the population on its small island empire doubled or tripled. So it instituted a birth control policy. Consequently, between 1949 and 1956 the population growth rate in Japan plummeted from 2.2 percent a year to scarcely 1 percent, a drop in fertility "unprecedented in the annals of world demography." Japan had in less than a decade accomplished what looked to be impossible, and all before the advent of modern contraceptives.

Two decades later China more than matched this. Between 1970 and 1976 it dropped its growth rate from 2.6 percent per year to 1.3 percent. In the 1980s it has tightened the lid on population growth another turn with its one-child-per-couple policy. The Chinese leadership collectivized the child-bearing decision in 1973, making a couple's family size a matter of public discussion. The aim then was replacement fertility—two children per couple on average, promoted by a policy of "late, spaced, and few." But looking closer at the situation, the Chinese saw ahead, for the 1980s, the coming of age of a flood of young adults entering the childbearing years. A two-children-per-couple policy would actually increase China's population by 50 percent, adding seven hundred million people—nearly the equivalent of another India—to what was already the largest population in the world. A further plummeting in the standard of living, already low enough, was the inevitable outcome. The nation's leadership adopted the strict one-child policy. It has not been easy, it has not been without its problems, and it could not work in every society, but the Chinese leadership believed it had little other choice.

Obviously, the Japanese and Chinese experiences could not be duplicated everywhere. Both, to a degree, were more heavy-handed than many nations would prefer. The size and nature of China, the rigidity of its society, its totalitarian government, all combined to shape its population policy. Most other societies are not—and do not want to be—like the China of the past quarter century. The coercive aspects of the Chinese policy are repugnant to me, and I believe to most people—especially those instances of coerced abortion. Concern over population growth ought not overwhelm all other values.

But the Japanese and Chinese examples nonetheless illuminate the possibilities. The world birthrate in 1988 was 28 per 1,000 population, lower than the 33 per 1,000 in both China and Japan before they launched their campaigns. With a serious effort it may be possible to lower the global rate to 19 per 1,000 by the

end of this century, a decline of one-third. This would cut the rate of population growth in half, dropping it to 1 percent a year. Much of this decline would have to be where present growth is so much out of control, in Africa, Latin America, and the Indian subcontinent. The growth rate in the industrial world—in the United States, the Soviet Union, Japan—is now under 1 percent, headed toward zero population growth.

The evidence is abundant that in nations that encourage birth control and give its people access to contraceptives, fertility drops. In Asian nations that established family-planning programs in the 1960s, including Indonesia, Thailand, and South Korea, crude birthrates over the past two decades declined by 25 to 60 percent. In Tunisia, birthrates fell twice as fast in the decade after its program was started as in the previous seven years. The birthrate in Mauritius was nearly 40 per 1,000 before 1965, when a birth-control program was started there. It dropped to below 25 per 1,000 in just the first eight years of the program. Mexico launched a program in 1973; its birthrate fell within four years from 45 per 1,000 to about 38 per 1,000. It is now down to about 31 per 1,000.

Countries that have successfully made the switch from big to small families share four common characteristics. They have an active national population education program. They have widely available family-planning services. They have incentives for small families, and in some cases, disincentives for large families. And they have widespread improvement in their economic and social conditions.

Over the last twenty-five years, birth control has gained acceptance in the less-developed countries. In the mid-1960s, only 10 percent of the populations of these countries lived under governments with aggressive birth-control policies. Today about 90 percent of such populations are under governments that support birth control.

However, the degree of support for these programs and their effectiveness vary greatly from nation to nation. Indonesia is an example of a nation that has lent birth control relentless support.

It officially launched its program in 1970. A decade later its National Family Planning Coordinating Board had established more than 40,000 village distribution centers for contraceptive devices and information, primarily in Java and Bali. Indonesia has tied these centers closely to agricultural cooperatives and health services, making them an intrinsic adjunct to its development efforts. The government has promoted the notion that a family should be "small, happy, and prosperous." It has backed this precept with an aggressive and pervasive program: an incessant bombardment of public messages about family planning, national family planning jingles that play when a train passes a railway crossing, and lectures on contraception at local mosques. At five o'clock every afternoon sirens wail to remind women to take their pill.

Since 1972, the fertility rate in Indonesia has dropped from 5.6 to 3.4 children per woman in the face of this public relations onslaught. While 400,000 Indonesian couples practiced birth control in 1972, by 1989 more than 18.6 million did. Abortion is illegal in Indonesia. The country has lowered its birth rate solely with strong government and community support, education, and the dissemination of free contraceptives to any couple who wants them.

Not all nations are that committed. Moreover, following the disaster of Indira Gandhi's forcible sterilization program in India, many governments are far more cautious.

Because of variations in government support, only an estimated one-fifth of fertile couples in less-developed countries (excluding China) actually practice birth control. Countries with birth-control programs saw their population growth rates fall on an average of 30 percent in the decade between 1965 and 1975. So, even at low use rates, there is apparently some impact.

If we wanted to reach replacement-level growth rates rather than simply curb high rates, an estimated 80 percent of fertile couples would have to use birth control. The cost of that, worldwide, would total from $5 billion to $8 billion a year.

At present, worldwide family-planning funds, including re-

sources from less-developed countries directly, are a little over $1 billion per year.

At current rates of program implementation, even with stronger government backing where it is not now aggressive, only about 50 percent of fertile couples are expected to be using birth control by the end of this century. This may make it difficult to stablize world population at 9 billion, a figure generally considered to be the absolute ceiling.

Five world regions have now reached stabilization or below-replacement levels of population growth (average 0.8 percent): Europe, the Soviet Union, Australasia, East Asia, and China. There are 2.3 billion people in these regions; 19 million are added each year.

Five other world regions are adding population at an average rate of 2.5 percent, 64 million persons each year: Southeast Asia, Latin America, the Indian subcontinent, the Middle East, and Africa. They are home to 2.6 billion persons.

Mortality rates, the problem at the other end of life, can be just as dramatically countered by making basic sanitary services and simple health care widely available. It is important to cut mortality rates, even in the face of an unwanted population surge, for many reasons. Among them are human compassion—particulary for the millions of young lives being lost. But another reason is the fact that while people strain the earth's carrying capacity, they are also its creative resource, and a potential asset in the coming environmental emergency. Only people can solve the problems their numbers create.

In the past, our concern about population growth centered on starvation. While that is still a powerful factor, there is now another consideration: We are at a point where human activity itself could destroy the resource base on which it depends—the planet's biological and chemical support systems.

It is in five world regions with the high population growth rates that the carrying capacity threatens to be exceeded. The populations in these countries are far more dependent on the

biological resources rather than fossil fuel energy for daily needs: fuel for cooking, wood for building, land for crops and livestock.

A 1985 World Bank study of seven West African countries found that they had already exceeded their carrying capacity for fuelwood by ten million persons, although their theoretical agricultural output would have supported an additional fifteen million.

Carrying capacity varies depending on which environmental element is in scarcest supply: In regions of poor energy sources, it is likely to be limited by lack of wood for fires as much as by shortages of land.

Despite the Green Revolution, the agricultural equivalent of the Industrial Revolution, farm productivity is being outpaced by population growth. In 1950, European grain production per capita was 515 pounds. African grain production per capita was 345 pounds. Although there is a difference, it is not that great in terms of overall nutrition.

In the thirty-five years between 1950 and 1985, total grain production rose 164 percent in Europe, and 129 percent in Africa. These were comparable improvements, stemming mostly from hybridization and increased use of fertilizer. But, because of population growth, by 1985, the per capita grain production figures were: Europe, 1,102 pounds; Africa, 330 pounds. The difference is that the European population rose 20 percent in that thirty-five-year span; the African population doubled.

Population growth has also increased landlessness. Although figures are hard to come by and are not always reliable (since governments claim virtues for their systems of land allocation), estimates are that in the Asian subcontinent (India, Pakistan, Bangladesh, and several smaller nations), 40 percent of rural households either lack land entirely or have less than one acre. Rarely can a family grow enough food on this little land to sustain itself. It is estimated that because of landholding patterns in Latin America, the percentage of landless is as high there—if not higher.

This landlessness is a major contributing factor to deforestation. Whether by governmental design (as in the Brazilian effort to "develop" Amazonia and solve some urbanization problems at the same time) or by individual human desperation (as in Indonesia, where deforestation is second to that in the Amazon), landless and unemployed people will use natural resources for their immediate needs.

The United States, which could be playing a constructive role in the population crisis and could be helping other nations curb their fertility rates, has chosen instead to export its domestic debate over the morality of birth control.

It could be increasing its direct funding for international family-planning resources. Instead, President Bush vetoed a bill in 1989 because it included $15 million that would have gone to UN population programs. The veto was shortsighted, induced by domestic political considerations. The U.S. Agency for International Development offers direct family-planning support to less developed countries outside the UN structure. This has risen from $120 million in 1972 to $220 million for fiscal 1989. However, the 1972 amount equals $239 million in 1982 dollars, so actual deliverable aid has dropped.

The U.S. could increase its government support for research and development. Private development of contraceptives is in decline, reduced by two factors. First, the Food and Drug Administration (FDA) testing requirements average a year longer for contraceptives than for other drugs (because contraceptive drugs are taken for a long time by otherwise healthy persons), which cuts into the seventeen-year patent life. Second, liability insurance and exposure is enormous in the wake of the Dalkon Shield case, in which a company was successfully and massively sued for a faulty and harmful contraceptive device. It is precisely because these drugs or devices are used for long time periods by otherwise healthy persons that liability can be so broad.

The U.S. could also lend a helping hand to private voluntary organizations overseas on the same basis that such organizations

can obtain funding within the United States. But we haven't. The Reagan administration perversely adopted (and the Bush administration has done likewise) a policy under which funds cannot go to private voluntary organizations in other countries if they use any of their own money to counsel for or provide abortions (not the U.S. money, *their own locally raised* money). Since private voluntary organizations are a principal source of birth-control information in countries where religious tradition creates obstacles to direct government programs (e.g., Latin America), the result is to effectively deny assistance to such organizations. In pursuing such a policy, President Bush is being incredibly shortsighted, especially since it appears to be a policy in which he does not believe, but which he has adopted for purely political reasons. He should—he must—reverse himself.

If we in the U.S. can lift our sights above our national prejudices and see the broader world need to stem the population tide that threatens to drown us all, our country can still play a valuable and pivotal role. It is another case in which we have the necessary financial and technical resources to help. All we need is the political will.

7

Unsafe
for Human Health

In early 1987, four prominent American doctors, three of them pediatricians, came to Washington and testified before my Senate subcommittee. In my opinion, what they said added an entirely new dimension to the debate on acid rain and the other pollutants poisoning our air. What they said was a foreshadowing of what is really at stake in the world environmental crisis: the lives, the health, and the well-being of our own species, and particularly our children—our Erics and Luisas. To convey the full impact of what was said I will take readers into the hearing room with me and recreate parts of that important testimony.

The hearing was held by the Subcommittee on Environmental Protection of the Senate Committee on Environment and Public Works. It convened that morning, February 3, 1987, at 9:30. I was presiding. Present were Senators Baucus of Montana, Graham of Florida, Chafee of Rhode Island, Stafford of Vermont, Durenberger of Minnesota, and Pressler of South Dakota.

I opened the hearing with a statement:

SENATOR MITCHELL: In the last few years there has been a great deal of research into adverse health effects of acid rain precursors

101

such as sulfur dioxide and nitrogen oxides. Today's hearing focuses on these effects.

Data suggest that sensitive populations, such as asthmatics,
experience increased ill-health due to existing, ambient levels of
sulfur dioxide.

A Harvard University study demonstrates that as levels of air
pollution increase, so do hospital admissions of children. In areas
like the Northeast, where there is cold weather and higher ambient
levels of sulfur dioxide, sensitive adults and children are more
vulnerable to wintertime illnesses.

These and other data demonstrate that the health risks associated with exposure to air pollutants may be greater than pre-
viously believed.

At a hearing last year, there was testimony that exposure to
sulfur dioxide and nitrogen oxides produces the same effects as
cigarette smoking. We have a national campaign against cigarette
smoking, and spend large sums of money to discourage people
from smoking, yet we do nothing to control these acid rain precursors. The effects are the same, but the administration's commitment is not.

The health data, when combined with actual damage to our
waters and potential damage to our forests, suggest that legislation
is needed. The fact that emissions of these pollutants are increasing
suggests that legislation is needed now.

When I introduced acid rain legislation six years ago, I was told
by the administration that more research was needed before congressional action was warranted. We have had research and the ironic
result is that the more research we do, the more the case for acid
rain legislation becomes clear, yet the administration's position is
that we need more research. In the December issue of the *EPA
Journal*, Lee Thomas, the administrator of the EPA, commenting
on the greenhouse effect and ozone depletion, said, and I quote:

"If we wait until health and environmental impacts are manifest,
it might be too late to take adequate steps to address these problems. We must realize that there will always be scientific uncertainty associated with these complex problems. We will have to
be prepared to act despite these uncertainties."

If that is an adequate standard for addressing this air pollution problem, surely it is the standard for addressing acid rain. I, for one, am prepared to act this year to pass acid rain legislation and invite the other members of the committee and the administration to join me.

The members of the subcommittee then welcomed the first witness, Dr. Richard M. Narkewicz, the president-elect of the American Academy of Pediatrics. Dr. Narkewicz has been a practicing pediatrician in Burlington, Vermont, for over twenty years. He was speaking for over thirty thousand fellow pediatricians who are members of his organization. And this, in part, is what he said:

DR. NARKEWICZ: The message is simple and to the point. It is hazardous to the health of children to breathe polluted air. Air pollution is a complex issue because the health effects depend upon many ingredients—the specific pollutant, the intensity of the dose and duration of the dose, and the specific characteristics of the patient involved.

The specific air pollutants of concern in this testimony, Mr. Chairman, are the oxidizing agents such as ozone and nitrous dioxide, and reducing agents such as sulfur dioxide. These are some of the ingredients of acid rain.

While the ecological, environmental effects of acid rain are much discussed, the focus of this testimony is that these pollutants contribute greatly to the development of human lung disease. These pollutants cause disease in children and significantly aggravate underlying respiratory conditions.

It is of great significance when you consider that pediatric pulmonary disease accounted for 21 percent of all hospitalizations in children under fifteen, and 29 percent of total hospital days in 1983. Combined figures from 1981 and 1982 indicate 4.5 million office visits. It is a staggering cost in morbidity and dollars.

The diseases we are talking about are asthma and bronchitis. These diseases can be caused or aggravated by many factors, especially air pollution. Children are particularly vulnerable to these pollutants. . . .

Number one, children's airways are much smaller than those of adults. The diameter of an adult bronchial tube is eight times larger than a child's bronchial tube. Therefore, you can easily see that breathing a pollutant that causes minor swelling and diminished diameter in an adult bronchial tube may produce dangerous obstruction in a child or infant.

Infants and children breathe more rapidly and, therefore, move more pollutant throughout the lungs. The repair process of children for damaged airways is less efficient than that of adults, and the immunologic immaturity of children contributes to more respiratory disease. The obvious risk is that children's exposure to pollution will be longer, because of their life span, which potentially exposes them to more long-term crippling events.

Mr. Chairman, I see many of these children with asthma and wheezy bronchitis in my practice. I consider air pollution in any child suffering from respiratory difficulty. Nowhere in medicine does the axiom "an ounce of prevention is worth a pound of cure" play a more dramatic role than in pediatric pulmonary disease.

I spend a major part of my time teaching the child and the parents to avoid the aggravating causes of asthma and bronchitis because once the wheezing and gasping has started, it is difficult to control, and usually leads to one or many office visits, often hospitalization, and sometimes death.

There is clear evidence that the underlying hyperreactivity of the small bronchial tubes of asthmatics, and those with bronchitis, are aggravated by pollutants such as the oxides of nitrogen, sulfates, and ozone.

In our role as practicing pediatricians, we are frustrated because we can't completely protect our patients from these irritants. Thus, we are forced to give our patients only symptomatic advice, which is the following: stay indoors at times of severe pollution; keep the room as cool as possible; use recirculated air if possible; no smoking in the home; and drink plenty of fluids.

Dr. Thomas Godar followed Dr. Narkewicz with some specifics. Dr. Godar, a practicing pulmonary physician, heads up the Pulmonary Disease Section at St. Francis Hospital and Medical

Center in Hartford, Connecticut. He is also associate professor of medicine at both the University of Connecticut School of Medicine and Yale University School of Medicine. He was speaking on behalf of the American Lung Association (ALA). He had been to see us before, but he was bringing new evidence:

DR. GODAR: . . . I appear before you today again with the very strong message that air pollution can and does have adverse impact on health. In some cases, this impact affects large populations. In 1981, the ALA encouraged the Committee to consider the need to strengthen the health protection measures of the [Clean Air] Act. Today, my message is the same but with greater urgency. The striking advances in information concerning health effects in the last several years justify this urgency. . . .

Witness the finding that healthy asthmatic subjects exposed to sulfur dioxide levels as low as 0.25 parts per million for exposure periods as brief as five minutes, when performing mild to moderate exercises, can develop symptomatic and objective evidence of bronchial constriction, that is a tightening of the airways.

Witness the finding that exposure to levels of sulfur dioxide found in the ambient air combined with exposure to cold dry air potentiate the onset of symptoms in as little as two minutes. These effects are of particular concern in areas such as the Ohio River Valley where such levels of sulfur dioxide and severe cold weather are common in the winter months.

Witness the finding that short-term exposures to 0.3 parts per million of nitrogen dioxide potentiates exercise-induced bronchial spasm and airways hyperreactivity in healthy asthmatic subjects. Cold air is also found to potentiate this effect.

Witness the finding that, when combined with intermittent heavy exercise, exposure to ozone levels as low as 0.12 parts per million can cause symptoms of airways irritation and decreased lung function in healthy subjects. These effects are reproducible in the same subjects when reexposed several weeks to one year later. In other words, there is reproducibility, there is no evidence of adaptation.

Witness the finding that exposure to 0.12 parts per million ozone in healthy subjects for a period typical of the normal workday . . . for persons employed in outdoor jobs, causes very significant decrements in lung function averaging reduction in forced expiratory volume in one second of half a liter. If your forced expiratory volume were four or five liters per second normally, this represents a 10 to 15 percent reduction in actual measurable lung function.

. . . we have documented that 20 percent of the population are sensitive to air pollutants, and there are health effects, if I could briefly list them. They are the pediatric population less than two years of age; pregnant women; patients with asthma, chronic bronchitis, and emphysema; patients with a history of myocardial infarction, angina pectoris, and other forms of coronary artery disease; and persons sixty-five years of age and older. . . .

Senators Baucus and Chafee followed Dr. Godar with statements. Then Dr. Anthony Robbins came to the witness table. Dr. Robbins is a past president of the American Public Health Association. He is also a former state health commissioner for the State of Vermont, a health director for the State of Colorado, and former director of the National Institute for Occupational Safety and Health. He was speaking for the fifty-five thousand public health professionals that comprise the American Public Health Association.

Dr. Robbins listed the direct effects of acid rain on human health: increased asthma attacks, increased acute respiratory problems, measurable decrements in pulmonary function, and particular problems for sensitive populations, young children, the elderly, those with respiratory disease, and those who have major exertion during work or exercise. Then he turned to the indirect effects.

DR. ROBBINS: The indirect effects are less well understood, but are becoming evident. Obviously, the acid rain has affected the trees, has killed many lakes, but there are other effects as people

consume the water from these sources because many of these lakes also serve as reservoirs. . . .

What happens when the water is acidified?

Acid water has the property of being able to leach certain metals from the soil, from the silt, and from the pipes through which it flows. We get lead, copper, and mercury, which may also be in the form of methylmercury and is more dangerous in terms of the health hazard put into solution. People have reported elevated aluminum levels as well.

We have a situation where these problems will continue and get worse as the presence of these acidified bodies of water leach more and more of these materials from the soil. At the present time, many public water systems simply add lye to the system and feel, at least, that they are protecting their old lead pipes, if they aren't changing the nature of these bodies of water.

What we also observe is that there has been more sensitivity in the health community, maybe because the remedy was more easily at hand, to doing something about toxic materials in water than in air.

Let me give you one brief example: We would close a water system if the public were getting the same levels of trichlorethylene [TCE] from the water that the public in many cities routinely receives from the air at the present time.

If you have one part per billion of trichlorethylene in the air, it is equal to five micrograms per cubic meter. If someone, a normal individual, breathes twenty cubic meters per day and absorbs 50 percent of the trichlorethylene in the air, or fifty micrograms per day, that would be comparable to consuming two liters of drinking water, which is the normal rate of consumption, with twenty-five micrograms per liter, 100 percent absorbed, or twenty-five parts per billion in that water.

Right now, the EPA advice on TCE in drinking water is that the maximum contaminant level should not exceed five parts per billion. So we have, from air exposures, situations where we are getting amounts that would not be tolerated in drinking water. . . .

The American Public Health Association believes there is suf-

ficient evidence, but you must convince yourselves that more than trees are dying from the pollution that causes acid rain. At stake are people's health and people's lives.

Dr. Robbins was followed by the final witness of the morning, Dr. Philip J. Landrigan, another pediatrician. Dr. Landrigan is professor of environmental medicine and professor of pediatrics at Mount Sinai School of Medicine in New York. He is also chairman of the Committee on Environmental Hazards of the American Academy of Pediatrics. In the mid-1980s he chaired a Committee on the Epidemiology of Air Pollution convened by the National Academy of Sciences. He put still more evidence on the table.

DR. LANDRIGAN: First of all, a word about current levels of pollutants. Levels of pollutants today are certainly lower than they were twenty years ago. In many respects, the Clean Air Act has been very successful. The so-called "killer fogs," such as that which occurred in Donora, Pennsylvania, are not seen any more in this country largely because of the good effects of the Clean Air Act.

On the other hand, the picture today is not uniformly benign. High local concentrations of air pollutants are seen still in relation to certain industrial complexes, and also along busy roadways. Sulfate concentrations are lower than they were in the past, but they are not negligible. In some parts of the country, particularly during the summer months, they rise to unacceptably high levels.

Perhaps most important, in terms of this morning's discussion, concentrations of ozone and of the oxides of nitrogen are not going down. In fact, there have been scattered increases in their concentrations over the past three to four years. . . .

There are several converging lines of evidence, all of which suggest that acid air pollution has adverse effects on the lungs of vulnerable people within our population, particularly on the lungs of children. . . .

One of the major studies on the health effects of air pollution is the so-called "Harvard Six-City Study," a study that researchers from the Harvard School of Public Health have been conducting over the past five years or so, following populations in six cities

across the country, which span the range in air contamination from very clean to quite dirty. They have measured concentrations of sulfate pollutants in those cities and they have serially examined lung function in children and in adults.

The Harvard researchers have found that exposure to acid air pollutants, especially to fine particulates and sulfates, causes increased respiratory disease among people in these cities. Children, for example, have increased bronchitis as concentrations of particulates rise in the air. Furthermore, the researchers point out that although children with a past history of asthma and wheezing are clearly the most susceptible to these effects, the effects are not restricted to those children. In fact, they are seen across the board to a greater or lesser extent in all children. . . .

Canadian researchers have found that in the summer months, as levels of ozone and sulfates rise, hospital admissions in children have increased dramatically and reproducibly year after year for the past eight years, such that at certain times of the year as many as 44 percent of hospital admissions in children in southwestern Ontario are caused by air pollution. . . .

These studies make the point that . . . changes in children's lung function are not just transient events that are here today and gone tomorrow. In fact, exposure to a few hours of severe air pollution at current levels can cause effects that last for at least a week.

These epidemiologic results are further corroborated by the results of studies that have been conducted on human volunteers in so-called "controlled chamber" studies. They are corroborated additionally by the results of animal experimentation where animals have been exposed to acid fog under test conditions. . . .

I would argue that in the present circumstances, the EPA cannot afford to wait, possibly for several more years, for more precise research data on the adverse effects of acid air pollution on the lungs. Good qualitative data and good semiqualitative data are available today. Considerations of cost and benefit pale, I think, when they are applied to the health of children. Any parent who sat by the bedside of a child with asthma would hardly consider cost-benefit issues.

The task confronting the regulatory agencies today is to exercise their mandate to protect not just the environment, but also the public health. I would argue that to await the completion of additional research before taking preventive action constitutes poor medicine, and it would constitute poor public policy.

When the four doctors had finished painting this composite picture of what acid rain is doing, particularly to young lungs, young bodies, and young lives, the senators began asking questions. I started it off with one question for all four witnesses: Did they believe that more stringent controls of emissions of sulfur dioxide and oxides of nitrogen are warranted now based on health considerations?

All four answered, yes—emphatically.

Dr. Godar added this elaboration:

We have no doubt . . . that precursors of acid rain are, indeed, hazardous. As a matter of fact, in the past, they have been major causes not only for morbidity, but for mortality. I would point out that the death of the human is a rather severe end point when one looks at cause and effect.

Morbidity is one thing. If the pediatric population has increased incidence of respiratory symptoms during childhood as a result of a pollutant such as sulfur oxides combined with particulates, and particularly with ozone, then let us consider that when that child grows up, the incidence of respiratory disease in adults will be increased, and the health care cost of that will be magnified.

It is very clear that when you have respiratory disease in children, you have respiratory disease in adults. We don't understand all of those mechanisms, but it means that the investment in safety for the pediatric population means investment in cost reduction for the health care in the adult in a very, very direct way.

Dr. Landrigan supported that statement with this one:

The recent epidemiologic evidence, the clinical evidence, and the laboratory evidence, all indicate that current levels of acid air pollution are responsible for increased respiratory disease in chil-

dren. They may additionally be responsible for increased risk of chronic lung disease in those same children as they grow to adult-hood. I think that these data constitute compelling reasons to [tighten] existing standards.

I then said what I have said many times since:

I think that this is a significant statement that I hope is noted beyond this hearing room, that here we have the four positions, the president-elect of the American Academy of Pediatrics, the president-elect designate of the American Lung Association, the past president of the American Public Health Association, and the director of Environmental and Occupational Medicine at Mount Sinai Medical Center in New York unanimously recom-mending to this committee or advising this committee that in their professional opinion, based upon their experience, that health considerations now represent a sufficient basis to justify legislation or action controlling emissions of sulfur dioxide and nitrogen oxide.

That is a significant development. Heretofore, the debate has focused entirely upon physical damage to our nation's waters, which has been clearly demonstrated, and potential damage to our nation's forests. This adds an important dimension to the debate on acid rain control.

Further important points surfaced as other senators continued to question the four doctors. A question from Senator Graham brought this exchange:

SENATOR GRAHAM: Could you assess how you would rank this in terms of the types of environmental and public health concerns which we, as the Congress, should be directing our attention toward? Is this in the upper 10 percentile of concerns for public health in America?

DR. ROBBINS: Senator, it is a difficult question. As the infor-mation comes in and the health effects of this kind of pollution become clearer, I think we can and will get some reasonable answers about the number of deaths, and what is happening.

It is probably less of a problem than smoking. It may be less of a problem than occupational exposures to toxic materials. But it is probably more of a problem than many of the other things that we are concerned about in society.

I think the thing that is important to recognize in relation to this pollution is that we do know how to reduce it. It is terribly important, when one is thinking about public health, to consider the solutions, and that they are available. Here one is available through reducing these emissions. So it is a solvable problem, and whenever we have death and disease caused in a manner that is preventable, it puts it higher on our list than some of the problems that we do not, right now, know how to solve.

Four months later in that same year Haluk Ozkaynak of Harvard's Energy and Environmental Policy Center, which had conducted the key study of the health effects of air pollution, testified before our subcommittee.

MR. OZKAYNAK: In every epidemiologic investigation that we have performed over the past six years, we have repeatedly found a 2 to 5 percent air pollution effect on human mortality and morbidity. We find it very difficult to reject these consistent findings, based on arguments sometimes raised about the possible influence of systematic errors or omitted confounding variables which may be uniformly biasing all of our results.

SENATOR MITCHELL: Did I understand you to say that in every such investigation over the last six years you found a 2 to 5 percent air pollution effect on mortality and morbidity? Is that what you said?

MR. OZKAYNAK: That is correct.

Mr. Ozkaynak was clearly telling us that acid rain kills. And not just lakes and trees. It kills people.

That, of course, was depressing enough. But also depressing to me is the fact that two years later some of these same doctors returned to our subcommittee. And nothing had changed except

the urgency of the problem (it had escalated) and the evidence (it was even more disturbing). There was still no acid rain legislation. And the administration was still saying the matter needed more study.

And I said, at the hearing in which Drs. Godar and Landrigan, joined by still others, repeated some of the same things they had told us two years earlier:

> I think it is very significant that the American people, through the press that are here, grasp the significance of what has been presented here today.
>
> We have been told by persons expert in the field, whose prior testimony has never been rebutted or even disputed, . . . that associated with air pollution in the United States and Canada are fifty thousand premature deaths each year, twenty-five million children at risk, a 25 percent increase in asthma in children, fifteen million elderly persons at risk, and health care costs of up to $40 billion each year due to air pollution.
>
> It is difficult for me to reach any conclusion other than that this is a public health emergency, an emergency of national scope and effect, requiring prompt and vigorous national action to deal with it. I think if every American parent comprehended the threat to his or her child from air pollution, they would overwhelm Congress with the demand for action.
>
> The only missing link is our inability to establish cause and effect between a specific source of pollution and a specific pollutant and the health of a specific child. We know in the aggregate what is occurring. A large number of sources emitting a large quantity of pollution are causing a large amount of damage to a large number of Americans. It seems to me that of all the testimony that we have received here on this subject, what we have heard of the effects on the health of the American people is the most important, the most compelling, and serves as the basis for action in this Congress.

Clearly it is my intention to see that action is taken. After all these years it is far past time. Moreover, the problem of acid rain,

its threat to human health and life, is but a cipher for the larger problem. As I have shown, human health is threatened as well by ultraviolet rays filtering through a shredded ozone layer in the stratosphere. Human lives may be threatened in ways we cannot now foresee by all of the forces that are likely to be unsheathed in a global warming of the magnitude that is currently being predicted. Who can tell what further dangers lie in store for the human species?

It is even clearer that other species are even more immediately endangered than ours. Everywhere on the planet, as I am about to show, their numbers are being decimated. And there is nothing these disappearing species can do to prevent their extinction. That too is in human hands.

8

Why the Songbird Is Important

The extinction of any species, no matter how lowly, how tiny, or how insignificant, is no small thing. Harvard's Edward O. Wilson has written in *Scientific American*:

> Virtually all ecologists, and I include myself among them, would argue that every species extinction diminishes humanity. Every microorganism, animal and plant contains on the order of from one million to ten billion bits of information in its genetic code, hammered into existence by an astronomical number of mutations and episodes of natural selection over the course of thousands or millions of years of evolution. Biologists may eventually come to read the entire genetic codes of some individual strains of a few of the vanishing species, but I doubt that they can hope to measure, let alone replace, the natural species and the great array of genetic strains composing them.

Nobody knows for certain how fast species are becoming extinct. It is probably safe to suggest that at least one of the earth's species is becoming extinct every day. One expert on the diversity of life has suggested the toll could be as high as one an hour. And even his estimate could be conservative. By the end of the

twenty-first century, even at the lower estimates, an appalling share of the earth's species may be forever gone. Even worse will be the anticipated extinction of entire genera and families of species. When a single species is lost there might be other close relatives left. But if whole genera and families are lost, nothing is left.

Wilson has called what is happening a "biodiversity crisis." He says:

> The human species came into being at the time of greatest biological diversity in the history of the earth. Today as human populations expand and alter the natural environment, they are reducing biological diversity to its lowest level since the end of the Mesozoic era, sixty-five million years ago. The ultimate consequences of this biological collision are beyond calculation and certain to be harmful. That, in essence, is the biodiversity crisis.

It is also impossible to know how many species of living things there actually are on earth. The closest we can come is by an order of magnitude. One estimate is 5 million to 10 million—as many as 30 million, if you count all of the insects. Only 1.5 million of these 30 million have been identified or studied. Recent research suggests that as many as 30 million insect species may exist in the world's tropical forests alone. If that is so, if treetops of the great rain forests are covered by such a vast living canopy, then we have no idea how rich the diversity of life really is. It means that there are in that great aerial cover thirty-four undiscovered insect species for every one known today. The Smithsonian Institution's Terry L. Erwin, whose studies of beetles in the rain forest has led us to accept such mind-boggling figures, believes that half an acre of Peruvian rain forest can contain over 40,000 species of insects.

But this teeming diversity could be wiped out overnight—is being wiped out—in the ecological holocaust now going on in the world's diminishing rain forests. Norman Myers, a noted British environmentalist, calls what is happening—this exter-

mination of species and its lost capacity for natural genetic regeneration—the death of birth. Scientists call it "ecosystem decay." Every one of them deplores it, because they consider the diversity of life on earth to be as important as the life itself. To lose that diversity, Dr. Wilson has said, "is the folly our descendants are least likely to forgive us." These scientists estimate, conservatively, that one in every one thousand species is now lost each year. If Erwin's figures are accurate, the toll could be far higher than that. A rate of extinction of one hundred species a day is not improbable.

Historic climate changes have obliterated species wholesale in the past. There is no reason to believe that the coming one, unmatched in world history in its expected scope, speed, or intensity, will not do far worse. The presence of humanity itself, a notorious killer of species—often inadvertently, sometimes knowingly—is likely to intensify the coming extinctions, absent an active preservation program.

The rate of extinction today compared to the historic norm through geologic time is awesome and terrifying. More species of the earth's plants and animals may be lost in our lifetime than in the mass extinctions that swept the dinosaurs from the earth sixty-five million years ago.

In the United States, which is species-poor by comparison with Madagascar, Ecuador, or South Africa, there are over 400 species of mammals, 460 reptiles, 660 freshwater fishes, tens of thousands of invertebrate species, and 22,000 plants. Some 650 species of birds either reside in the U.S. or pass through every year. About 495 of these species are currently listed as endangered. Over 2,500 other species await consideration for that dubious status by the U.S. Fish and Wildlife Service. The list is dominated by plants, birds, fish, and mammals, but it includes insects, amphibians, reptiles, mollusks, and crustaceans.

Until recently the small island nation of Madagascar, which holds one of the earth's richest rain forests, contained 9,500 documented plant species and an estimated 190,000 animal spe-

cies. Sixty percent of these species were to be found only in Madagascar. Ninety-three percent of that forest is now gone, and with it 60,000 species. If the last 10 percent of this forest is razed, imagine the life that will be lost.

The forests of western Ecuador are said once to have contained between 8,000 and 10,000 plant species, with corresponding numbers of animal and insect species matching the wealth of life in Madagascar. Half of those species were found only in those forests. In the past thirty years the entire forest cover has been stripped away. Imagine the life that has been lost.

Some 6,000 known plant species inhabit just one ten-thousand-square-kilometer section of South Africa's Cape Floristic Kingdom. Seven of ten of these thousands of plant species are found nowhere but there. That plant kingdom is now threatened. Imagine the life that could be lost.

Russell E. Train, chairman of the board of the World Wildlife Fund, a former EPA administrator, and long one of America's environmental leaders, has warned that if we continue mindlessly destroying the great rain forests, we may, "without firing a shot . . . kill one-fifth of all species of life on this planet in the next twenty years."

The world's rain forests are literally "cradles of life." They hold 40 percent of all the species on earth, and are the hothouses for most of the world's plants. And the pace of their obliteration matches the destruction of the forests themselves.

If, by the year 2000, 15 percent of these plant species become extinct, who knows what we will have lost? Who can say what obscure species that becomes extinct in our next scything of a rain forest might have held the genetic key to the next great medical miracle? We simply can't afford to lose some inauspicious life-form that may be, without our suspecting it, the cure we have been desperately seeking for AIDS or cancer or another of humankind's prime killers. Of the 250,000 plant species on earth only 1 in 10 has been investigated in even a cursory way to assess its usefulness to humanity, only 1 in 100 in any detail.

The rain forest, as the world's hothouse, is also its leading source of medicines for the curing of human ills, for plants are the healers of humankind. Without the bark of the aspen, which yields the glucoside called salicin, there would be no aspirin, today proving such a powerful antidote to heart attack and stroke. Without the lowly mold, a species of fungus, there would be no healing penicillin. Forty percent of all medical prescriptions in the U.S. derive from plants. And the tropical forests, disappearing now at a rate of an acre a second, are the preeminent source. The rain forests are the sole origin of quinine, the most potent bulwark against malaria. They are the sole source of the Madagascar periwinkle, from which we draw one of our most powerful present weapons against leukemia and Hodgkin's disease. Thirty years ago, a sufferer from leukemia faced a one-in-five chance of remission. Two drugs from the rosy periwinkle have upped the odds of survival by four times. The worldwide sale of these two drugs, drawn from this moist tropical forest plant from Madagascar, is now more than $100 million a year. Abdus Salam of Pakistan, a Nobel Laureate in physics, tells us that tropical deforestation is leading to the loss of $20 billion every year in medically essential species.

More than 1,300 plant species from the rain forests have been used by the Amerindians as medicines. Traditional healers in southeast Asia use 6,500 different plants as treatments for malaria, stomach ulcers, syphilis, and a host of other ailments. Some 1,400 plant species from the rain forest are believed to possess properties effective against cancer.

There is a another side to the extinction coin. Some species may benefit—at least initially—from this holocaust in the biosphere. Some species of fish in some systems, such as the Great Lakes, may see their vistas grow. Others may be able to migrate to new habitats as they open up farther north. But fish in the small lakes and streams, locked in and unable to escape temperatures beyond their tolerances, may simply perish as their habitats vanish. We also know enough about how things work to un-

derstand that when life returns to habitats where it has been lost, it may not return as it originally existed—either in the richness of numbers or the richness of form. Often the species that return are the ecological opportunists that seem to survive extinction spasms—the weedy plants of life, the rats, the cockroaches, the carp, the house sparrows, and the starlings.

"It is possible, even probable," Norman Myers has written, "that within fifty years, when many current species disappear and their places begin to be taken by others, we will have a disproportionate number of species we would characterize as 'pests' or weed species. That is the kind of biological world our children are going to have to contend with."

The wanton wasting of single species is not the whole picture. The overriding, mystifying fact of life on earth is its vast and complicated interrelationships. While no single species may be essential to the normal functioning of the biosphere, all species together are, as a noted American ecological scientist has said, the "driving force that maintains it." "The world's most important resources," George M. Woodwell of the Woods Hole Research Center has written, "are biotic—the plants and animals that maintain the biosphere as a habitat suitable for life."

Moreover, if one species is threatened in an area rich in life, such as a rain forest, then perhaps thousands of other species unknown to man may be sharing the same fate. Woodwell believes that hundreds, perhaps thousands of other species, conceivably including whole genera yet unnamed, may already have been lost as the forests have disappeared in the wake of human intrusion.

It is this pervasive human intrusion into the ages-old workings of the natural world that has caused the problem. And it is that human intrusion that must now be reined in if we are to survive. We must curb wanton human disruption of the plant and animal world as surely as we must curb the outpouring of the greenhouse gases, the CFCs, and the precursors of acid rain into the atmosphere. "There are thresholds," the World Commission on En-

vironment and Development told us in 1987, "that cannot be crossed without endangering the basic integrity of the system. Today we are close to many of these thresholds; we must be ever mindful of the risk of endangering the survival of life on Earth. Moreover, the speed with which changes in resource use are taking place gives little time in which to anticipate and prevent unexpected effects."

Again, Rachel Carson has been our oracle. In *Silent Spring* she talked of ". . . the impetuous and heedless pace of man rather than the deliberate pace of nature." She wrote that "it took hundreds of millions of years to produce the life that now inhabits the earth—eons of time in which that developing and evolving and diversifying life reached a state of adjustment and balance with its surrounds. . . . Given time—time not in years but in millennia—life adjusts, and a balance has been reached. For time is the essential ingredient; but in the modern world there is no time."

Our industrial and chemical revolutions have triggered no less than a biotic hemorrhage on the planet over the last century. Even as we have seemed to have enriched life with our wonder chemicals and our industrial marvels, we have been impoverishing it. Scientists such as George Woodwell know how this works. Every acre of life-rich forest that gives way to pasture or grassland or crops or, worse, desert, commonly reduces the production of biomass (the total amount of living matter in the area) by 50 percent—or more. As Woodwell explains it, the destruction of forests and their replacement by shrubs reduces not only the diversity of life, but also the net production and therefore the potential for supporting life.

The immediate demands of a swelling population to divert primary production of life into human food—an understandable drive in a world where starvation is all too common—collides directly with the need to maintain the biosphere as a rich and versatile caldron of life.

The diversity of this caldron of life is what gives the biosphere

its necessary balance. The ongoing disruption of that balance has become global, where before it was only regional. Global climate change on the scale we can now foresee will cause unprecedented continuing disruption that is difficult to predict, still more difficult to cope with. The certain outcome, however, will be further impoverishment of the planet. It will set off a chain of changes that will touch all living things and destroy many of them, leading to a biosphere that is less and less capable of supporting life—including human life.

"Normal operation of the biosphere," Woodwell has written, "is dependent on the normal operation of its parts, not species alone, but whole units of the earth's surface. The normal function is biotic, follows simple rules, and requires no tinkering by man. Disturbed chronically, problems accumulate. Current trends are toward the destruction of these systems, toward drastic alteration of their function, and toward equally drastic changes in the biosphere that will diminish its habitability for man."

If Woodwell is right, and if we are dangerously close to stepping over thresholds that must not be crossed, then the immediate priority is to preserve the normal functioning of biotic systems that are the basic components of the biosphere. In short, we must stop interfering. We must stop killing species. That doesn't mean we must stop being productive and striving for a high standard of living. It does not mean that the human species itself can't or shouldn't be in these fragile ecosystems. But it does mean that we must do the right things while we are there. It does mean that we must interfere with life systems as little as possible. It means we must hit on a balance that permits us to live decent lives without impoverishing the world and our future in the process. We must recognize the need to rein ourselves in, to control the use of the earth's surface to assure that biotic diversity is fostered and maintained.

To find ways of doing that is a monumental challenge. Humankind has never faced a greater one. We cannot continue our way of life. It is too dangerous to all species, including our own. It

will no longer be acceptable. Certain acts of the past—detonation of nuclear weapons within the biosphere, control of pests with persistent toxins—are simply not acceptable. To these we must now add still others—control of the outpouring of greenhouse gases in the atmosphere, a halt to the chemical mayhem we have caused, an end to the destruction of life in the rain forests, an end to the biotic hemorrhage that is also of our making.

If Soviet President Mikhail Gorbachev is to be believed, we can expect strong Soviet cooperation in confronting this challenge. Speaking to a Global Forum of Spiritual and Parliamentary Leaders on Human Survival in Moscow on January 19, 1990, he said:

> The great minds of the past foresaw the consequences of the thoughtless "conquering" of nature by man. They warned that humankind could kill itself by destroying the vegetable and animal kingdoms and poisoning the earth, water, and air. At the end of the twentieth century, we have a very acute crisis in relations among man, society, and nature. Paraphrasing Immanuel Kant, it is safe to say that the ecological imperative has forcefully entered the policy of states and people's everyday life. It is becoming unconditional, and not only because perhaps irreparable damage has been done to nature. The new scientific, technical, and technological revolution, all the consequences of which we do not know yet, can make this damage irreversible. As distinct from some absolute pessimists, we are not fatalists. But the hour of decision—the hour of historic choice—has come, and there is no reasonable alternative for man because he is not predisposed to suicide.

"Humanity is a part of the single and integral biosphere," Gorbachev said in that same address. "The stability of ecosystems, and hence, the quality of the environment, depend on the preservation and maintenance of biological diversity and equilibrium of the biosphere. . . .Something should be substantially changed in the factors for further progress in order to ensure man's initial right—the right to life."

The stakes in the coming struggle to contain global climate change are no less than extinction, not only of the lower life-forms that make our medicines, but ultimately of humanity itself. And extinction, no matter on what level, is irrevocable and irreversible. Rachel Carson warned us more than two decades ago that our songbirds were dying from the effects of pesticides and herbicides in the food chain. Will the epigraph for the species lost in the coming global warming say simply: Died in a disaster not of their own making? It is clear to me that when we let the songbird die, when we let species become extinct, we foreordain our own extinction.

The ultimate risk, in not stemming as best we can the headlong gallop of these Four Horsemen of global environmental change, is to turn the world into a lifeless desert. After extinction there is nothing. There is no computer, no ingenious mechanism, no sleight of hand that can recreate even one of the lowest forms of life when it is wiped from the face of the earth. We are in grave danger of losing forever the world's priceless genetic heritage in the coming crisis. It is our duty to see that this does not happen, that the songbird and all other life threatened with it, live. To fail in this will be an unforgivable dereliction of our duty to our planet, to ourselves, and to our children and their children.

And it will be something we will forever regret. As Harvard's Wilson has written:

> In one sense the loss of diversity is the most important process of environmental change. I say this because it is the only process that is wholly irreversible. Its consequences are also the least predictable, because the value of the earth's biota (the fauna and flora collectively) remains largely unstudied and unappreciated. Every country can be said to have three forms of wealth: material, cultural, and biological. The first two we understand very well, because they are the substance of our everyday lives. Biological wealth is taken much less seriously. This is a serious strategic error, one that will be increasingly regretted as time passes.

SAVING THE PLANET

Had I been present at the creation, I would have given some useful hints for the better ordering of the universe.

ALFONSO THE WISE

9

Can It Be Fixed?

In October 1987 President Maumoon Abdul Gayoom of the Republic of Maldives went before the United Nations General Assembly and announced that his country was an "endangered nation."

Gayoom's remote 1,196-island state occupies nineteen coral atolls stretching for five hundred miles out over the North Indian Ocean from Sri Lanka. It lies helpless in the path of the coming environmental crisis. No part of it stands more than six feet above sea level. By the end of the next century, in a warming world, it could become more and more uninhabitable in the face of a rising sea and, like the uncounted species in the rain forests, face extinction. It was not surprising to hear Gayoom say in the light of this that "the predicted effects of the change are unnerving."

His words were both an indictment of the industrial world that had doomed his nation and a cry for it to redeem itself by redeeming his country. "We did not contribute to the impending catastrophe to our nation," he told the General Assembly, "and alone we cannot save ourselves."

Can anyone now save the Maldives? Is it too late to save even ourselves? A warming of the earth has already been set in motion. We are committed to it. A resulting rise in sea level in the next

century is inevitable. The question is how soon and how much, and do we still have time to do something about it?

I believe we do. Admittedly, great damage has already been done, and we appear to be heading into a crisis that will hit with full fury in the first half of the twenty-first century. The changes it brings are likely to persist for centuries. The lifetimes of some of the greenhouse gases are very long. The ozone-piercing CFCs that are already in the stratosphere or headed there will persist for a century or more. It may take many centuries to regenerate our lost tropical forests. And lost species can never be recovered. But if we can't stop global environmental change—and we can't entirely—at least we can try to slow its pace and buy ourselves precious time to deal with its effects. I believe that to be possible.

Three key energy policy specialists at the Congressional Office of Technology Assessment (OTA), John H. Gibbons, Peter D. Blair, and Holly L. Gwin, also believe it possible. In their article "Strategies for Energy Use" in the *Scientific American* of September 1989, they wrote:

> We can change the story. Technological ingenuity can dramatically reduce the amount of energy required to provide a given level of goods and services, simultaneously cutting down on energy-driven problems. Investments in energy efficiency can help us reduce fossil-fuel demand without sacrificing economic growth. Application of existing efficiency technologies can save investment capital, buy time for the development of new supply technologies, and ultimately make it possible to provide a higher level of goods and services at a given level of energy consumption.

U Thant, the late secretary-general of the United Nations, said in 1969 that the inhabitants of the world "have perhaps ten years left" to improve the human environment. If environmental problems are not addressed soon, he said twenty years ago, then they will have reached such staggering proportions that they "will be beyond our capacity to control." Professor Roald Sagdeyev of the Soviet Academy of Sciences has since said, "The crime has been

committed but we still may, if we're astute, escape some of the sentence."

I agree. There is still time.

But we must begin now. We must act. The four-decade chemical experiment we have been conducting on our planet and on ourselves and all living things must be controlled. We must now use our great knowledge and resources to save ourselves.

It will not be easy. As Lincoln told the Congress in the midst of another great crisis more than 135 years ago, "The dogmas of the quiet past are inadequate to the stormy present." The world can save itself—and, hopefully, the Maldives—but only with an unprecedented mobilization of resources and a new attitude by the political leaders and the people of all nations. The war against global environmental change calls for scientific and political co-operation on a scale that the world has never seen. The challenge to science, technology, and diplomacy will be enormous.

As I hope I have made clear, the coming environmental crisis will itself be unprecedented. It will be far different, of far greater enormity, than the pollution crisis of twenty years ago, for the problem has escalated by many magnitudes and eclipsed every national boundary. It has been said that air pollution problems and their consequences are in the true sense of the term boundless.

The two pioneering atmospheric chemists, Drs. Graedel and Crutzen, have also written in the *Scientific American* of September 1989:

> We and many others think the solution to the earth's environmental problems lies in a truly global effort, involving unprecedented collaboration by scientists, citizens, and world leaders. The most technologically developed nations have to reduce their disproportionate use of the earth's resources. Moreover, the developing countries must be helped to adopt environmentally sound technologies and planning strategies as they elevate the standard of living for their populations, whose rapid growth and need for increased energy are a major cause for environmental concern.

With proper attention devoted to maintaining the atmosphere's stability, perhaps the chemical changes that are now occurring can be kept within limits that will sustain the physical processes and the ecological balance of the planet.

Mostafa Tolba, the executive director of the United Nations Environmental Program (UNEP), believes that "the option facing governments at this time is stark: take action or face certain disaster." He told UNEP's Governing Council meeting in Nairobi in May 1989:

> In global warming and ozone depletion, destruction of forests, extinction of wild plant and animal species, expanding desertification, shortage of fresh water, ocean and coastal problems, hazards posed by toxic wastes, and potentially dangerous chemicals, human society faces a challenge unprecedented in ten thousand years of civilization. To deal with this crisis, the peoples and governments of the world will have to engineer common and concerted action . . . on an unprecedented scale.

Engineering such common and concerted action on such a scale is, like the magnitude of the warming itself, beyond human experience. Reaching international agreement to act in consort on such a far-reaching matter could be painfully slow. Treaties could take years to shape, sign, and ratify—the better part of a decade in the best of circumstances, perhaps longer. Gathering necessary scientific knowledge to assure that we make the right decisions could take a matter of decades. The U.S. Environmental Protection Agency tells us that a large menu of promising technologies have been identified that can still meet our needs and lower greenhouse gas emissions. But many of these take time, often many years, to bring to market. And once they are on line it may take more years to win a large market share and still more years for the existing capital stock to be replaced. It could take twenty to fifty years or more to substantially alter the technological base of industrial societies to meet this emergency. It would take the developing nations less time, because they have

less to change. For both rich and poor it will be expensive at first, but energy-saving and cost-saving in the end.

It could be 2010 or beyond before there is vigorous concerted international action, and, of course, still longer if we do not act now. The earth, meanwhile, will have committed to still more warming—half again as great in just those 20 or 30 years as what has been committed to in the entire 125 years of the industrial age. A global warming of somewhere between three to nine degrees Fahrenheit by 2030 seems reasonable, no matter what we do. Even as we try to come to a common mind against this common menace, the greenhouse clock will continue to tick.

The issue is not stopping the world from warming at all. That isn't now possible. Some warming has been locked in. The challenge now is to slow the production of the greenhouse gases as soon as possible, to slow future warming, to avoid if we can the most sudden and catastrophic climate changes. And the first requirement, the overriding priority, is to create nationally and internationally a heightened sense of urgency, a driving awareness that this must be done. The danger signals are flashing world-wide, lighting up scientific monitoring systems everywhere. They must be heeded and taken to heart.

The obstacles, even to this necessary acknowledgment, are formidable. Too many in the past have refused to listen and heed. They have discounted the warning signs. They have argued—and some still do—that there is too little data, too little knowledge of the long-term effects of global climatic change. They have argued that we must await further scientific study. Proper scientific data is certainly essential, and the picture of what the world faces is still uncertain. But we can no longer wait for scientific certainty. Although study must continue, and on a crash basis, we can't wait for a clearer picture of the crisis. It is already too painfully clear. And as Daniel Arap Moi, the president of Kenya, said so succinctly nearly a decade ago, "Time is not on our side." That is even more true today than it was then.

In the face of all the evidence that things are going terribly

wrong on the planet, the only prudent course is prevention. We cannot gamble with the future of our world. The longer we wait the greater are the odds against us. The effort will be costly—into the many billions of dollars—but the costs of not acting will be far greater. The risk of taking action is now outstripped by the far greater risk of doing nothing. For all our sowing, we are now reaping a whirlwind. We must try to diminish its fury.

Rallying the Nations

Nearly two decades ago, in June 1972, the United Nations held a conference on the human environment in Stockholm. It was an environmental milestone, the first time in history that environmental decision-makers from the highest national levels had ever met to consider the issue. It was an acknowledgment that the environmental problems threatening all nations in common are urgent—and must be dealt with.

It was an acknowledgment by the world community that the whole notion of international security as traditionally understood must change in the face of this overriding common challenge. It was a tacit recognition of the idea—to come into full flower in the late 1980s—that political and military threats to national sovereignty must be expanded to include this threat that knows no borders. And it was an admission that solutions must be of a different kind altogether. There are no military solutions to the kind of environmental insecurity the world now faces. As another secretary-general of the UN, Kurt Waldheim, said on the occasion of the Stockholm conference, "No political system preserves us from this threat; no level of economic development permits escape. We are all equal in the face of the danger—equally threatened and equally vulnerable."

"International economic security is inconceivable," Mikhail Gorbachev told the UN General Assembly two years after Gayoom's passionate plea, "unless related not only to disarmament but also to the elimination of the threat to the world's environ-

ment. In a number of regions, the state of the environment is simply frightening."

He has since been even more explicit. In his address to the Global Forum of Spiritual and Parliamentary Leaders on Human Survival in Moscow in early 1990, he said that the threat of a military thermonuclear catastrophe has been joined by "a second threat, the assessment of which until recently was clearly inadequate to its gravity—the threat to life on Earth as a result of damage to the environment."

Gorbachev, like Gayoom, speaks of the threat from firsthand experience. The USSR is one of the prime contributors to the problem—and one of its most stricken victims. The Soviet Union contributes a fifth of all the world's CO_2 emissions to the atmosphere, second only to the U.S. It also contributes a fifth of its SO_2 and a tenth of its CFCs. Numbing pollution can be found throughout the country, levels that are off the chart, exceeding legal limits in some parts of the nation by factors of up to one thousand. The Soviet environment has paid dearly for industrialization.

The Soviet leader admitted "that in the Soviet Union we only recently came to understand the vital importance of the ecological problem to a proper extent at the level of policy. The war danger stood in our light." He said with great candor: "Perestroika has also altered our views on ecology."

The environmental devastation in the Soviet Union has been matched, perhaps surpassed, in the other Communist bloc countries. That has become strikingly evident since the secrecy that hid such things from world view has evaporated in the new political reforms that have swept Eastern Europe. The *Wall Street Journal*, reporting from Budapest in March 1990, indicated that "the new access to government data has brought disclosures suggesting that outmoded technology and a dependence on the cheapest fuels caused pollution at levels almost unimaginable in the West."

The *Journal* said scientists and doctors believe that as many as

10 percent of the deaths in Hungary are directly related to pollution and that it is probably even worse in parts of Czechoslovakia, Poland, and East Germany. A seventy-five-year-old woman waiting in a Budapest lung clinic for her turn at a fifteen-minute stint in an "inhalitorium," a telephone-booth-size closet where people come to breathe clean air, said: "In this part of the world, nobody takes breathing for granted."

Eastern European countries emit more than seventeen million tons of sulfur into the air every year, the equivalent, the *Journal* said, of five million loaded dump trucks. Emission levels per square mile are almost seven times as high as in the U.S. As in the Soviet Union, Eastern Europe had many strict environmental laws on the books. But for decades industrial production was simply more important. The environment was ignored, neglected, and abused—to a near-catastrophic extent.

Gorbachev is saying things now about the environment nearly as revolutionary as what he has been saying about the Communist economic and political system—and promising reforms as dramatic. In his address to the Global Forum of Spiritual and Parliamentary Leaders on Human Survival he spoke of the "ecologization of politics." And he said:

Ecologization of politics means a new look at the problem of consumption and its rationalization. People's living standards should not be raised by exhausting natural resources. This process should be accompanied by a restoration of the living conditions of the animal and plant world.

Ecologization of politics affects the methods of handling many social problems, especially damage to people's health as a result of damage to the environment.

Ecologization of politics implies all possible support for scientific research and fundamental studies of the biosphere and its ecosystems.

Ecologization of politics requires acknowledgement of the priority of universal human values in making ecology a part of education and instruction from early age, molding a new contem-

porary attitude to nature and, at the same time returning to man a sense of being a part of nature. No moral improvement of society is possible without that.

The Soviet leader announced that a detailed report on the ecological situation in the USSR had recently been published, the first in the history of the Soviet state. He said "we have already begun a major overhaul of the entire system of nature conservation in this country," and that work was almost completed on a draft of a national long-term program for environmental protection and the national use of natural resources. "In other words," he said, "we are to exert great efforts to harmonize our relations with nature."

If anything is going to shape the world's nations into one people, it is the threat now facing the common environment. There are signs that the crisis is already beginning to shake the sanctity of individual national sovereignties like nothing else has ever done. The world is at a point where only international instruments, wielded cooperatively by all nations in concert, can cope with the problem.

We are clearly on the threshold of an age in which environmental alliances—nations uniting against the common ecological enemy—will become as important as military alliances. Such alliances are already forming. A group of European nations and Canada in 1985 united in a "30 Percent Club" in which they pledged together to scale down their SO_2 emissions by at least 30 percent by 1993. They have since been joined by other nations. Another alliance of European countries was launched in 1988 to cut NO_x emissions by 30 percent. Environmental alliances have also sprung up around the North and Baltic seas. In 1987 the eight nations bordering the North Sea agreed to reduce their nutrient and toxic discharges by half by 1995. A similar accord has been signed by the seven Baltic nations. A major environmental alliance was forged in Central America in 1988 —an agreement by Costa Rica, El Salvador, Honduras, Nica-

ragua, and Panama to establish "peace parks." Under it the nations agreed to preserve their common rain forests and promote
sustainable development. These parks could perhaps become a
world model for sustainable tropical forest development.

Bilateral environmental agreements are beginning to emerge.
More than one hundred have been signed between East and West
European nations. West Germany is a party to seventy or eighty
of them. For West Germany this is more than enlightened self-
interest. It is virtually an act of self-survival, for the spillover of
pollution from its eastern bloc neighbors could potentially devastate its own environment. A recent study comparing air quality
in East and West Germany showed sulfur dioxide readings in
East Germany to be typically six to thirteen times higher than in
West Germany. *The Wall Street Journal* reported that on a cold
day at six in the evening in Mölbis, a small village south of
Leipzig, scientists measured sulfur dioxide levels that in a West
German city would have required evacuation of the entire pop-
ulace.

East and West Germans have agreed to pay jointly for desa-
linizing the Werra, a border-crossing river. The two German
states also signed a Basic Environmental Agreement in June 1987
to deal with their mutual air pollution, forest damage, and water
quality problems. West Germany has also entered an agreement
with Czechoslovakia to pay for some SO_2 scrubbers for the Czech
power plants that are sending acid rain over the border.

But the ultimate need is for concerted world action, for an
environmental union of all nations. For the war against global
climate change and stratospheric ozone depletion will ultimately
be fought not on a bilateral or even a regional battlefield. It will
be fought worldwide. The seeds of a worldwide union against
this common enemy are starting to be sown. The Montreal Protocol, a union of more than thirty nations—now grown to over
sixty—to scale down CFC emissions, has pointed the way. And
the United Nations Environmental Program (UNEP) and the
World Meteorological Organization (WMO) have now joined

to launch a third body, the Intergovernmental Panel on Climate Change (IPCC), to begin to deal with the broader crisis.

Three IPCC working groups have been at work. One chaired by the United Kingdom has combed the scientific evidence to determine if a global warming trend has really begun worldwide and, if so, to assess its causes. A second, chaired by the USSR, has been considering the environmental, economic, and social impact of climate change. A third, chaired by the United States, has been charting a response to the crisis. These three working groups were to issue reports in the summer of 1990. Their conclusions and recommendations were to be presented to the panel's parent bodies in the fall of 1990. An international convention on climate change, leading ultimately to a world accord, a Law of the Air Treaty or something similar to the accord now governing use of the seas, may be the next logical step.

A basic national precept that may become a dinosaur in this forced uniting of nations against a common environmental enemy is the traditional primacy of military security. It may simply find itself overwhelmed by a larger crisis.

The Soviet Union has called for a massive effort to shift world resources from military security to environmental security. Mikhail Gorbachev, in his address to the Global Forum of Spiritual and Parliamentary Leaders on Human Survival, said:

> The Soviet Union believes that the time has come when the limitation of military activity is needed not only for lessening the danger of war but for protecting the environment. The best thing to do here would be to ban all nuclear tests. . . . I reiterate the Soviet Union's readiness to ban nuclear tests completely, for all times, and at any moment, if the U.S. does the same.
>
> The convention on and the prohibition and complete elimination of chemical weapons which, we hope, will be signed soon, misses the need to ensure an ecologically safe method of accomplishing this task. Here, too, international cooperation would be extremely welcome, for we are going to eliminate tens of thousands of tons of these lethal weapons. Generally speaking, military

activity on land, in the air, and in the seas and oceans, and even in outer space—should be run with due account taken of its ecological consequences. With this end in view we are planning to introduce certain limitations on the flights of military aviation, and on the movement of the land forces and of warships. We are also prepared to sign international agreements on this score.

One Third World general has said: "The soldier now comes to another front, the environmental front." And an American writer, Wendell Berry, has written: To what point do we "defend from foreign enemies a country that we are destroying ourselves? In spite of all our propagandists can do, the foreign threat inevitably seems diminished when our air is unsafe to breathe, when our drinking water is unsafe to drink, when our rivers carry tonnages of topsoil that make light of the freight they carry in boats, when our forests are dying from air pollution and acid rain, and when we ourselves are sick from poisons in the air."

The nations of the world collectively by the end of the 1980s were spending astronomically—over $900 billion a year—on military security, arming themselves against one another. That is more than $2.5 billion every day of the year. The United States was spending a third of that total. The military threat is always with us and must be dealt with. But the environmental threat is now also with us and is perhaps an even greater danger. And with far less than that kind of money, it could be dealt with:

- A proposed Action Plan for Tropical Forests would cost $1.3 billion a year, half a day's worth of military security, over five years.

- Implementing the UN Action Plan for Desertification would cost $4.5 billion a year, less than two days of military spending, over two decades.

- The lack of clean water for human use, which causes 80 percent of the diseases in the Third World and is dooming its children to an early death, could have been adequately dealt with during the 1980s at a cost of $30 billion a year, the equivalent of twelve days of military spending.

- We could clean up ten thousand of the worst hazardous waste dumps in the U.S. for $100 billion, forty days of military security.

- We could pay for two-thirds of the cost of meeting all of U.S. clean water goals by the year 2000 with only twenty-five days of military spending.

- Germany could clean up its sector of the North Sea for little more than four days of military spending.

- The U.S. could cut its SO_2 emissions by eight to twelve million tons a year with two and a half days of military funding.

- The U.S. could pay for all of its efforts to increase energy efficiency with less than two days of military security.

- A solar power system for a city of two hundred thousand could be built for less than two days spending, about what is being spent on research for the Strategic Defense Initiative.

- For less than two days of military spending, the hazardous waste sites in ten European countries could be cleaned up by the turn of the century.

- For the cost of one Trident submarine, half a day's military funding, a global five-year child immunization program against six deadly diseases could be conducted, preventing an estimated million deaths a year.

These urgent environmental security problems, and others with them, could be funded for less than the world's nations now spend every year protecting themselves from one another.

Any such broad-scale diversion of money from military to environmental security would, of course, be enormously dislocating, requiring a major conversion. An estimated fifty million people, soldiers and civilians, are on military payrolls around the world. An untamed environmental crisis, however, would be even more dislocating, affecting far more people.

Another even more basic precept about nationhood, individual sovereignty, is also undergoing change. Some of it may have to

be modified in the face of the coming crisis. Canada's Tom McMillan has said that "the challenge ahead is for us to transcend the self-interest of our respective nation-states so as to embrace a broader self-interest—the survival of the human species in a threatened world."

Another Canadian, Maurice F. Strong, the secretary-general of the Stockholm conference, said in 1972:

> The dominant image of the age in which we live is that of the earth rising above the horizon of the moon—a beautiful, solitary, fragile sphere which provides the home and sustains the life of the entire human species. From this perspective it is impossible to see the boundaries of nations and all the other artificial barriers that divide men. What brings it home to us with dramatic force is the reality that our common dependence on the health of our only one earth and our common interest in caring for it transcend all our man-made divisions. In the decades ahead, we must learn to conquer our own divisions, our greeds, our inhibitions, and our fears. If we don't, then they will conquer us.

Ten years later, at another international meeting in Nairobi to mark the tenth anniversary of the Stockholm meeting, Strong urged a "new earth ethic" in which "our competitive drives are more disciplined by our communal instincts and our propensities for cooperation. It must be one in which respect for each other's needs and aspirations constrain our individual self-indulgence and in which conservation and caring for earth's precious resources replaces extravagant consumerism and wasteful and destructive resource use."

The Rich and the Poor

The nations that now must assume a leading role in trying to stem the environmental crisis are the industrial countries—the rich nations of the world, made rich at the prohibitive cost of imperiling the planet in the process. They include the United States.

They account for three-quarters of all greenhouse gases now threatening the environment. They have had their day in the sun. The poorer nations can say, with some justification, "OK, you've doubled the concentration of CO_2 in the atmosphere and made a good life for your people. Now it is our turn." Barring workable alternatives, they are going to go the same route the rich have gone, with their own massive outpouring of greenhouse gases into the atmosphere. The rich nations must now reach out to the poor with their technology and try to help them, if it is possible, to reap the benefits of an industrial world without using—and abusing—the same sources of energy. It won't be easy. But we must try.

The world's poor are very hard on the environment; they have little choice, and you don't have to be rich to be wasteful. Neither regulation nor taxes are likely to deter them from polluting the world in the traditional way to reap its benefits, barring an alternative that is just as good. What the Third World wants are the energy levels of the industrial world. Only with such levels of energy can the developing nations meet their peoples' needs. Their aspirations are justified. But the energy it would require by the year 2025 would simply devastate the planet, if that energy comes from traditional sources. The ecosystem couldn't stand it. It would amount to ecocide. The danger of global warming and the acidification of the environment rule out even a doubling of energy use based on the present mix of energy sources.

Despite this, China has blueprinted an ambitious industrialization program that would nearly double its coal consumption in the next decade. Its present path of industrial development could make it the premier emitter of CO_2 into the atmosphere of all the nations, including the U.S. It is already the third biggest burner of fossil fuels behind only the U.S. and the Soviet Union. By 2025 it may be the largest emitter of CO_2 in the world. No other nation would pollute the environment so dramatically.

China's energy profligacy is rooted in its large and growing population (the largest on earth), its tendency to use energy-

intensive processes, its poor energy efficiency, and its unrelenting reliance on coal. Between 1980 and 1986 manufacturing grew by 12 percent a year in China, the fastest growth of any large nation in the world. It has a lot of room to grow more energy efficient.

Scenarios today predict that all of the developing nations together will draw even with the industrial world in greenhouse emissions by 2025 and will be outstripping them by a ratio of 3 to 2 by the end of the twenty-first century.

All of these nations aspire to standards of living for their people that such polluting now implies. Jim MacNeill, the secretary-general of the World Commission on Environment and Development, has written in *Scientific American* that "a fivefold to tenfold increase in economic activity would be required over the next fifty years in order to meet the needs and aspirations of a burgeoning world population, as well as to begin to reduce mass poverty. If such poverty is not reduced significantly and soon, there really is no way to stop the accelerating decline in the planet's stocks of basic capital: its forests, soils, species, fisheries, waters, and atmosphere."

He says further:

A fivefold to tenfold increase in economic activity translates into a colossal new burden on the ecosphere. Imagine what it means in terms of planetary investment in housing, transport, agriculture, and industry. If current forms of development were employed, energy use alone would have to increase by a factor of five just to bring developing countries, with their present populations, up to the levels of consumption now prevailing in the industrialized world. Similar factors can be cited for food, water, shelter, and the other essentials of life.

An increase in economic activity by a factor of from five to ten sounds enormous, but because of the magic of compound interest, it represents annual growth rates of only between 3.2 and 4.7 percent. What government of any country, developed or developing, does not aspire at least to that? Indeed, such rates are

hardly enough to keep up with projected population growth in developing countries.

If Third World nations cannot be restrained from filling the atmosphere with greenhouse gases, as the industrial nations have done, then the next best thing may be for the rich nations of the world to set a goal of halving their CO_2 emissions by 2020 to make room for Third World growth without it ending in a complete environmental disaster. Even so, the earth will grow substantially warmer. Without help the industrial world cannot now reverse the damage it was able to do alone.

The Third World doesn't have to pollute at industrial nation levels to grow. One analysis shows that the best energy technology available today could give a developing nation a mid-1970s European level of energy services and increase energy consumption by only 20 percent over the average consumption of a developing country in 1980.

The rich industrial nations have perhaps the most to lose in the coming climate change. Australia and New Zealand, for example, lie beneath the widening rift in the Antarctic ozone layer. The Netherlands with only its celebrated dikes and dunes now holding back a normal sea, stands to go under in the higher seas of a global warming unless it acts. It has in place now a comprehensive National Environmental Policy Plan designed to make its environmental problems manageable within the next twenty to twenty-five years. To keep its program on track, that water-threatened nation has called for a reevaluation and updating of its plan every four years beginning in 1994.

To millions of the world's poor, simple survival overrides every other consideration. As an Egyptian delegate to the Nairobi conference said in 1982, "What might be considered as a necessity for some people is a luxury that cannot be afforded by others. The individual who has to walk a mile or two each day to get fresh water is not concerned with the protection of a certain plant or insect species. The people who do not have a shelter from the

hot and damp weather do not care much about wildlife reservations. The millions who suffer from malnutrition cannot be concerned about a newly discovered chemical that causes gene mutation in a species of mice."

It will be necessary, whatever else happens, for the nations of the world to strike a global balance so that a slowing of earth warming and economic development can coexist. One key to this may lie in debt-for-nature swaps—forgiveness of debt in underdeveloped nations in return for projects that protect the forests and develop local economies in sustainable ways. The raw materials for such bargains are there. The cumulative debt of developing countries has now surpassed $1 trillion. The annual interest payments alone approach $60 billion. And the fifteen tropical countries of Latin America, Asia, and Africa that contain virtually all of the world's major rain forests are also among the world's major debtor nations.

Such debt-for-nature swaps are beginning to happen. The U.S. Agency for International Development struck an agreement with Madagascar in August 1989, the first of its kind by an American institution. Most of Madagascar's lush forests have already been lost. Perhaps now the destruction of the island's remaining two hundred thousand plant and animal species, many of them unique to its rain forests, can yet be averted. Without a conservation effort they and the diversity of life within them stand to disappear early in the next century.

A world goal of rehabilitating 370 million acres of seriously degraded tropical watersheds and preserving 250 million acres of threatened forest ecosystems is not unreasonable. But it is possible only if we can strike more such deals with other developing nations with endangered environmental resources. It is possible only if we can improve and expand industrial forestry programs, and vastly upgrade forestry research, education, and training worldwide. Farmers in the developing world must be helped with technology, materials, and credit. Innovative ways of helping village cooperatives, governments, and private com-

panies use but not waste the forests must be devised. Large tracts of the world's rain forests must be put out of the reach of the chainsaw and the torch. Many experts have suggested that at least 20 percent of tropical forests should be protected. But today less than 5 percent has protection of any kind; many of the tropical forest parks still exist only on paper. Future settlement must be channeled into unforested lands and buffer zones created on the fringes of the forests themselves. Less wasteful logging methods and better forest management practices must be encouraged.

There are some hopeful signs that some of these things are starting to happen. Much of it is happening on the lowest levels—with people within their local environments. Individuals armed with iron resolve and some technological help can do a lot to save the environment, even to bringing back dead lands and staying the march of the advancing deserts.

The First Step: Doing It More Efficiently

There is no panacea, no miracle cure-all in dealing with the environmental crisis that will make everything right. But the closest thing we have to one, and the most immediately accessible first step in that direction, is good old-fashioned efficiency. We can be far more efficient than we are with energy. We can respect it more, and we can conserve it. And we should be bending every effort worldwide to do that.

Energy experts assure us that much of the technical sophistication necessary to save enormous amounts of energy already exists. Compared with the costs of fossil fuels and the capital costs of new supplies, they are often far cheaper as well.

What is needed now are several things. We need more government and privately funded research to push ourselves past existing technology limits. We need to intensify the development and application of energy sources and supplies that are renewable year after year and decade after decade. Many of these technologies—solar, wind, thermal, geothermal—are available

now and competitive. While these sources at first can only complement fossil fuels, ultimately they must replace them. Meanwhile, until that happens, the answer must be greater efficiency to hold down the demands on fossil fuels. Efficiency can lessen environmental problems, save investment money, and eventually give us the same standard of living on less energy.

None of that is possible, of course, without political will. As the trio of policy experts from the Congressional Office of Technology Assessment (OTA), one of them a scientist, one an engineer, and one a lawyer, have written, "policy adjustments to foster efficiency will require that we plow through some new emotional territory." As they point out, political will is also crucial "for exploiting some alternative-energy technologies."

This must be done. These alternative-energy sources must be pushed. But even as we do that we can begin being more efficient with the energy we use. And we can begin virtually where we sit.

In buildings, for example. In 1985, buildings in industrialized countries consumed almost as much energy as OPEC produced. More energy passes through the windows of buildings in the U.S than flows through the Alaska pipeline. This exorbitant demand could be sharply reduced simply with new condensing furnaces. Such furnaces reabsorb much heat from exhaust gases; therefore they need 28 percent less fuel and they emit fewer pollutants into the atmosphere than conventional gas furnaces. Moreover, systems are available to control the indoor environments of buildings by monitoring outdoor and indoor temperatures, sunlight, and the location of people, and beaming light and conditioned air only where they are needed. That can save 10 to 20 percent on energy. A combination of improved lamps, reflectors, and daytime lighting could cut the consumption of energy for lighting in buildings by more than 75 percent.

In homes, advanced building materials can sharply lower loss of heat through windows, doors, and walls. The trio from the OTA point to "superinsulated" homes, where normal insulation

is doubled and a liner forms an airtight seal in walls. In this super-sealed environment, heat radiating from people, light, stoves, and other appliances alone can warm the house. Such super-insulated homes in Minnesota require 68 percent less heat. In Sweden similar homes are saving 89 percent of the energy.

In industry, energy consumption can be dramatically lowered with improvements in industrial motors, sensors and controls, advanced heat-recovery systems, and friction-reducing technologies. For instance, cogeneration, the production of heat and electricity together in the same process, can save vast amounts of energy. Only a third of the energy from the steam produced by a boiler in a conventional electric-power plant is converted to electricity. A cogeneration plant could channel much of the remaining energy in the used steam as a heat source for other jobs. In the paper industry, efficiency can be sharply heightened by automated process control, greater process speeds, and high-pressure rollers. In the steel industry, advanced processes can save 40 percent of the energy now spent; in developing nations the savings can be even more dramatic. China and India now use four times more energy to make a ton of steel than Japan does.

In the utilities industry, fluidized-bed combustion, in which burning coal is suspended in a stream of air, can both increase efficiency and reduce pollution. The aero-derivative turbine, based on jet engine designs and burning natural gas, can raise conversion efficiency in electric power generation from its present 33 percent to more than 45 percent.

In transportation, which constitutes the largest and most rapidly growing drain on the world's oil reserves and is such a threat to the environment, the opportunities for efficiency are as striking as the opportunities for waste. Cars and light trucks consume one out of every three barrels of oil used in the U.S. and account for 15 percent of the country's CO_2 emissions. Use of lighter materials, radial tires to reduce rolling resistance, fuel injection, variable speed transmissions, and redesigned exteriors to decrease aerodynamic drag all hold promise. They have already markedly

improved the efficiency of new cars and trucks over the last fifteen years. Such innovations as continuously variable transmissions and direct-injection diesel engines are also noteworthy energy savers. The technology to push automobile fuel economy over sixty-five miles per gallon already exists. Right now, with existing technology and little cost to consumers, new-car fuel economy in the U.S. could be increased to thirty-three miles a gallon. Increases in fuel efficiency will not only reduce emissions of carbon dioxide, but emissions of hydrocarbons and carbon monoxide as well.

The savings in energy across the board if all or most of these readily available innovations were embraced would be striking. They would go a long way in rescuing the planet from its descent into environmental chaos.

But as I have suggested in my earlier discussion of rich nations and poor nations, and as Gibbons, Blair, and Gwin have clearly said, "even dramatic improvements in energy efficiency will not be sufficient to protect the environment if they are confined to the industrialized world. Economic projections show that if nothing is done to hasten energy-technology development and to move existing efficiency technologies into the market in developing countries, global climatic change and other major environmental problems will escalate beyond acceptable bounds."

Gibbons, Blair, and Gwin calculate that even if industrialized countries managed to halve their carbon dioxide emissions, population growth and economic development in the less-developed countries would most likely drive annual worldwide emissions of CO_2 to 2.5 times what they are today.

They also suggest "it may be up to more industrialized countries to encourage—through technology transfer, subsidies, or loans—policies or technologies that take developing countries beyond the levels of efficiency justifiable on the basis of free-market prices. Such policies would require unprecedented levels of international cooperation."

They believe it would be worth the effort. To quote them more fully:

> But it is the collective response of developing countries to opportunities for efficient resource use in their economies that will determine humanity's ultimate success in slowing the deterioration of the global environment. New technology can help less-developed countries to leap over the undesirable practices of the past and follow new energy paths for development. The industrialized world and developing countries must work together to ensure that opportunities are available and, when sensible, are accepted. Investment in energy-efficiency technologies, which often cost the same as the fuels they displace, represents the most sensible energy path available today. The challenges are great, but so are the opportunities.

The Bottom Line: A Sustainable World

In 1983, the United Nations General Assembly called for, and caused to be created, the World Commission on Environment and Development. It was chaired by Gro Harlem Brundtland, who went on to become the prime minister of Norway.

After a thorough, three-year study that tapped environmental and economic expertise worldwide, the commission came to this basic conclusion: The needs of those persons now living (all five billion of them) could be met in a way that does not deprive those who will be living in the next century (all ten billion of them) of their ability to meet their needs only if a policy of sustainable development is pursued worldwide. According to its secretary-general, Jim MacNeill, the commission defined sustainable development as "new paths of economic and social progress that 'meet the needs of the present without compromising the ability of future generations to meet their own needs.' " If stated in monetary terms, it would mean living off interest without dipping into capital. It is a formulation easy to preach, but exceedingly difficult to practice.

As William D. Ruckelshaus, a commission member and the former administrator of the EPA, has pointed out, sustainability was once very much in fashion. It was the original economy of our species. "Preindustrial peoples," he says in an article on a sustainable world in *Scientific American*, "lived sustainably because they had to; if they did not, if they expanded their populations beyond the available resource base, then sooner or later they starved or had to migrate. The sustainability of their way of life was maintained by a particular consciousness regarding nature: The people were spiritually connected to the animals and plants on which they subsisted; they were part of the landscape, or of nature, not set apart as masters."

It was when humans began to view themselves as masters of all other forms of life on earth, even the forms that had long died and become fossilized, that the environment began to suffer. Sustainability gave way then to what Ruckelshaus calls "transitional unsustainability."

That is what most modern economies practice today. They borrow recklessly from the future to pay for the present. An American need look no farther than the fiscal policies of the eight years of the Reagan administration for evidence of this. The man who spent twelve years running for president so he could balance the budget, proposed and presided over the most unbalanced budgets in our nation's history. "Tax and spend" was replaced by "borrow and spend," with a vengeance. As a result, in those eight years the debt of the United States increased twice as much as it did in the entire previous 192 years of our national history.

The mode of thinking induced by such policies was expressed, if inadvertently, by one senator during a closed session of the Senate Finance Committee. When asked about the effects beyond 1994 of a proposal he was advancing, he replied: "That's the future. It's too far away to worry about. My concern is with the present." Unfortunately, he has not been alone in regarding anything more than five years off as a vague "future," "too far away to worry about."

Not only must we change our way of thinking, we must encourage others to change theirs as well. We will be subject to the charge that we are asking others to do as we say, not as we've done. We must accept the rebuke as accurate and move forward undaunted.

It is of critical importance that the less-developed countries adopt and pursue policies of sustainable development in the coming decades. For it is there that population growth, and hence pressure for immediate and unrestrained development, will be greatest.

The Worldwatch Institute recently identified those targets which would be essential in any effort to achieve a policy of sustainable development. They included "slowing population growth, protecting topsoil on cropland, reforesting the earth, raising energy efficiency, developing renewable energy, and retiring the debt of developing countries." While intended to apply worldwide, these targets are plainly most applicable and most needed in the Third World countries.

Ruckelshaus, the former EPA administrator and member of the World Commission on Environment and Development, has cogently described the route to a policy of sustainable development in his *Scientific American* article:

> Although we cannot return to the sustainable economy of our distant ancestors, in principle there is no reason why we cannot create a sustainability consciousness suitable to the modern era. Such a consciousness would include the following beliefs:
>
> *1. The human species is part of nature. Its existence depends on its ability to draw sustenance from a finite natural world; its continuance depends on its ability to abstain from destroying the natural systems that regenerate this world.* This seems to be the major lesson of the current environmental situation as well as being a direct corollary of the second law of thermodynamics.
>
> *2. Economic activity must account for the environmental costs of production.* Environmental regulation has made a start here, albeit a small one. The market has not even begun to be mobilized to

preserve the environment; as a consequence an increasing amount of the "wealth" we create is in a sense stolen from our descendants.

3. *The maintenance of a livable global environment depends on the sustainable development of the entire human family.* If 80 percent of the members of our species are poor, we can not hope to live in a world at peace; if the poor nations attempt to improve their lot by the methods we rich have pioneered, the result will eventually be world ecological damage.

This consciousness will not be attained simply because the arguments for change are good or because the alternatives are unpleasant. Nor will exhortation suffice. The central lesson of realistic policy-making is that most individuals and organizations change when it is in their interest to change, either because they derive some benefit from changing or because they incur sanctions when they do not—and the shorter the time between change (or failure to change) and benefit (or sanction), the better. This is not mere cynicism. Although people will struggle and suffer for long periods to achieve a goal, it is not reasonable to expect people or organizations to work against their immediate interests for very long—particularly in a democratic system, where what they perceive to be their interests are so important in guiding the government.

To change interests, three things are required. First, a clear set of values consistent with the consciousness of sustainability must be articulated by leaders in both the public and the private sector. Next, motivations need to be established that will support the values. Finally, institutions must be developed that will effectively apply the motivations. The first is relatively easy, the second much harder, and the third perhaps hardest of all.

The most significant aspect and most difficult problem in winning acceptance for a policy of sustainable development is in agriculture. It is the crucible in which sustainability will be tested, and in which the fate of the world environment will be decided.

Western agricultural practices require a high level of inputs. They call for plowing vast amounts of energy and capital into machinery, chemical fertilizers, and pest controls. The rewards

of this approach under existing climatic conditions are high production. But the price is also high—perhaps too high: some of high-input's byproducts are devastating the environment.

The most obvious byproduct is nonpoint-source water pollution, that which comes from no single pipe or other pinpointable source—rainwater or irrigation runoff, for instance. In the U.S., the states are developing plans for control, as required under recent amendments to the federal Clean Water Act. However, since the act bars federal implementation of the plans, even when they are inadequate, it is uncertain at this time whether the law will work.

There are other problems: consumer objections to chemical residues on food, groundwater contamination by chemical agents (EPA has already found seventy-four pesticide residues in the groundwater of twenty-six states; a more thorough review is now under way), and overuse of erodible lands. But these problems have received relatively little attention.

Irrigation is now widespread throughout the American West. But it is also costly. The cost of irrigation and the salinization it brings with it to the soil (as well as the competition for the water itself) have made it a storm center of U.S. farm policy. Federal water is subsidized in the West, and this has led to some overproduction and overlapping subsidies: Some of the subsidized water is used to grow crops which are in surplus and for which price supports are therefore available.

An effort should be made to encourage users of subsidized water to upgrade their irrigation systems where feasible to make them more appropriate for dryland farming. Systems that deliver the water to the plant, rather than spraying it into the air, where as much as 75 percent of it evaporates, are well known and used extensively in water-short countries such as Israel. If we are going to subsidize water for irrigation in places where water is scarce, the least we should do is require that it be used with some concern for conservation.

Better irrigation techniques (i.e., using less water) would also

reduce the salinization that is occurring on California farmlands. Soils and water systems at the end of irrigation runs in that big farm state are developing high concentrations of mineral salts, which poison the soil and harm adjacent wetlands.

A five-year American Academy of Sciences study suggests that funding for research on low-input, sustainable agriculture be raised to $40 million.

Low-input farming means less tilling (therefore less exposure of soil to water and wind erosion); less reliance on herbicides and pesticides and more reliance on integrated pest management—such as putting one insect in the field to devour another and timing harvests to avoid pest life cycles; and less use of chemical fertilizers, relying instead on a mixed-farm approach in which intercropping, crop rotation, and animal fertilizer again figure in the farm cycle.

Low-input farming is attractive to some farmers because it costs less. Although yields are somewhat lower, net farmer income often stays the same because the costs are lower. Lower yields are perhaps a reflection of over-hybridization, in that specialized plants sometimes lack the resistance to insects or drought that the original wild plant enjoyed. (Research could, for instance, focus on development of plant types best suited to non-chemical farming.)

Low-input farming's potential importance to Third World economies cannot be overstated. For the general public, such practices would mean no farm chemicals to taint its food, its water, or its air. This would bypass the costs at both the pollution end and the regulatory food-safety end. It might also save in human health-care costs, and in lives. The savings associated with this benefit have not been factored into traditional farming equations; perhaps it is time that they were.

No-till cropping at the same time saves tractor fuel and reduces erosion. It takes about a century to develop one inch of topsoil. As the Dust Bowl of the 1930s showed, ten centuries of natural development can vanish in less than a decade under poor management.

The fact that Dust Bowl–era farmers are gone and are no longer farming the land has meant that their insistence on windbreaks and more careful management of the soil has been overshadowed by more modern concerns. So when the federal government told farmers to plant fence-to-fence, many of them, for whom the Dust Bowl held few memories, ripped up the hedgerows that had been planted in the 1930s. If we get a few years of successive drought in some midwestern areas, wind erosion could again ravage the land. It might even be inevitable in a world that is three to nine degrees warmer than today.

Intercropping and crop rotation have been replaced since 1945 with monoculture farming—the same crop year after year. Monocultures unfortunately invite a high development of weed and insect pests that attack the unchanging crop. This in turn begets the well-known cycle of higher applications of pesticides followed by more resistant pest populations, followed by yet more pesticides. It becomes a dangerous and vicious circle.

The smaller, more mixed-farming enterprises that are part of the low-input concept are particularly well suited to regions such as the Northeast, where larger tracts are rare. A substantial resurgence of such farming would preserve open land near urban centers and reduce transportation costs for vegetable crops. The system of the past, which existed when the hinterlands were the primary food sources for nearby cities, cannot be reestablished entirely. But that system possessed benefits that have been lost in the current practice of trucking enormous loads of perishable food across the entire continent.

The U.S. government has been managing agricultural prices for most of this century. The focus in recent years has been on exports. But that may not be the proper focus in the coming century of climate change. It would be well, therefore, to begin refocusing now, rather than under the pressure of rising temperatures and shifting rainfall patterns.

In the U.S., interest in sustainable agriculture has caught on in part because of recent farmer disenchantment with the high costs of chemicals. It is being increasingly viewed as a return to

traditional farm practices rather than as an exotic idea pushed by city dwellers fleeing back to nature.

Worldwide, the barriers to environmentally sustainable farming are more formidable and more severe: population pressures that lead to overgrazing, shortages of funds for even modest technological improvements in irrigation, governmental policies that favor low food prices in urban areas and thus impoverish rural dwellers, and expansion onto marginal lands.

From 1950 to 1976, cereal cropland worldwide expanded from some 1.4 billion acres to over 1.7 billion, a 22 percent increase. Major increases were in the U.S. and Brazil, following urgent demands for grain from the Soviet Union and India in the early 1970s. In the face of that demand, U.S. grain area rose by about a tenth.

The area of grain land in the Soviet Union, however, has contracted by about 12 percent overall. In China, where a Maoist campaign to increase grain production collapsed, the croplands shrunk by about a tenth from 1976 to 1986.

In the U.S., the collapse of farm prices in the early 1980s led to a farm income crisis. That in turn triggered the sodbuster/ swampbuster provisions of the 1985 farm bill (which pays to restore marginal lands to grass or wetlands) and encouraged the continued high rate of farm price supports. The goal of the 1985 act is to reduce U.S. cropland by about one-seventh.

Irrigation is responsible for more than half the harvest gains from the Green Revolution. In 1900, there were about 98 million irrigated acres worldwide. By 1950, there were 230 million. By 1986, there were 620 million. Two-thirds of this area is in Asia, which is one of the reasons the continent can support half the world's population.

The combination of expanding to marginal lands and of irrigating otherwise dry lands has several outcomes. Marginal lands are more susceptible to water and wind erosion. This lowers the productivity of the soil and brings on heavier and heavier applications of fertilizer to maintain yields. Intensive irrigation can

lower water tables (making deeper wells necessary, thereby requiring more pumping power), waterlog dry land where the subsoil is impermeable, and concentrate salts. This creates a wholly new problem because mineral salts are dissolved from the earth. Plant roots ordinarily take in water by osmosis, but in the presence of salts, they tend to lose water by the same process. This means that more irrigation is needed to maintain the plant, more dissolved salts are delivered, and we have another vicious circle. Plants have different tolerances for salts. But only desert vegetation can grow in land where salt concentrations are abnormally high. Some farmlands in particularly sunny areas, such as Pakistan, India, China, the U.S., and the USSR, have had to be abandoned because of salinization that makes growth impossible. Some 148 million acres—nearly a quarter of the world's irrigated land—is damaged by salinization.

Aquifer depletion is best known in connection with the Oglala Aquifer in the U.S. Problems are also developing in China, India, Mexico, and elsewhere. It may indeed be a widespread problem, but it is difficult to tell for certain because for the most part groundwater aquifers are still insufficiently mapped.

Use of chemical fertilizers per capita quintupled worldwide between 1950 and 1986, from 14 million to 131 million tons. This offset the loss of per capita cropland by about one-third. At the beginning of this period, grain response to fertilizer was impressive: 624 million tons of grain produced with 14 million tons of fertilizer, a ratio of 46 to 1. By 1986, 131 million tons of fertilizer produced 1,660 million tons of grain, a ratio of only 13 to 1. The diminishing-returns problem also contributes to pollution: As much as one-fourth of fertilizer is lost to runoff or leaches past plant root zones, and so is not taken up.

Agriculture has become a voracious user of energy in this century. Overall, including fertilizer, the equivalent of 276 million barrels of oil were consumed in farming in 1950; by 1985 total use reached 1.9 billion barrels. The rate of growth has slowed, however, in this past decade, reflecting both the strains

that have beset farm income and the huge debt that has gripped the Third World.

Average grain yields around the world are now 5.6 tons an acre. If food demand grows 2 percent a year until the end of the century, yields would have to rise to 8.5 tons per acre in the absence of more croplands or another Green Revolution break-through. This may be achievable. But it could require substan-tially more energy.

A World Bank survey in 1980 examined nutrition levels world-wide. At that time, excluding China, 730 million persons received less than 90 percent of the World Health Organisation's nutrition standard (a caloric level at which growth is not stunted, but people cannot perform at full capacity). One hundred fifty million were in sub-Saharan Africa, the rest in the Indian subcontinent —two of the most environmentally vulnerable regions of the world.

This level of nutrition was a percentage improvement from 1970. But population growth in the meantime had raised the actual numbers of persons at this low nutritional level from 680 million to 730 million by 1980. The number is now estimated at about 800 million.

The same World Bank survey found 340 million persons (since risen to about 400 million) received under 80 percent of the caloric standard (a level that tends to stunt growth and damage health). Half of these were in India, a quarter in sub-Saharan Africa. The rest were scattered in smaller nations, typically where per capita income is $400 a year or less.

The most useful thing our government can do to help resolve this problem is to lend its considerable research and technology skills. Given that new Green Revolution breakthroughs seem unlikely (and there may not be the money to sustain high-cost agriculture), the focus should be on improving traditional crops. Techniques such as agro-forestry (where reforestation and crop growing are carried on together) can help deal with several prob-lems at once—fuelwood, water retention, erosion control, and food production.

Most advanced biotechnology research is now in the hands of private companies and focused on high-value crops. Therefore, if the traditional food crops are to get attention, governmental researchers are probably going to have to do it.

Better distribution of soil-enhancing fertilizers would also help. Much fertilizer today is wasted. Western high-intensive farmlands lose (to leaching and runoff) as much as 160 pounds of fertilizer per acre, which is more than an acre of cropland ever gets in many Third World countries.

We can do better in creating a sustainable world. The coming environmental crisis requires it of us. It is another element of the problem that will more and more demand our attention and our best technological talent. And it will require the participation of all people. As the melancholy man in the White House in 1862 wisely said, "Neither significance nor insignificance can spare any one or another of us."

10

Rising to the Occasion

As people around the world have begun to look about them and to see where our planet is headed environmentally, they have begun to act. They have begun to act in the international arena. They have begun to act in countries, in cities, and in neighborhoods. They have begun to act in their congresses and in their legislatures. There have been successes and there have been failures. There have been breakthroughs and there has been foot-dragging. But above all there have been efforts. In this chapter I will chronicle some of these efforts. They constitute only a beginning of what must be done.

The Miracle at Montreal

Two dozen nations in 1987 signed an accord in Montreal to curb the emissions of CFCs into the atmosphere by half. Pushed hard by the U.S., particularly by two Americans, Richard Benedict on the government side and David Doniger in the environmental community, and brokered by the United Nations, it was a giant step, an unprecedented accomplishment, the first truly global treaty ever signed to deal with a threat to the environment.

161

But even as it was taking effect in January 1989 with many more nations signed on, a serious call was going out to amend it, to make it even stronger, to end the production and use of CFCs entirely by the end of this century. The miracle at Montreal, as unique as it was, was simply not good enough.

The CFCs offer the very best opportunity for dealing with world climate change. They are not only one of the most serious threats to the environment, but the most controllable. Yet even with the Montreal Protocol the concentration of chlorine compounds in the atmosphere could triple by the middle of the next century, as CFCs now in use leak out into the atmosphere, as new uses for these wonder chemicals are developed and as demand for them quickens in the undeveloped nations. But since CFCs are wholly made by man, they are also within man's means to control. If all now-known control measures were implemented today, total CFC and halon emissions could be cut by 90 percent. Many of these control measures are already within the world's reach economically. And compared to the cost of the damage these chemicals, so benign on earth and so lethal in the stratosphere, do to the environment, controls are dramatically cost-effective.

The heartening fact is that many nations in the world see this. That made the Montreal Protocol possible. To our credit, the United States was a major participant and one of the original ratifiers. As originally drawn after long months of negotiation, the signing nations agreed to halve most CFC emissions by 1998 and freeze halon emissions by 1992. Fortunately, these are synthetic chemicals for which substitutes might be developed. Under the protocol there was to have been a freeze by 1989 on CFC production at 1986 levels, a 20 percent decrease by 1993, and another 30 percent decrease by 1998. Halon production will be frozen at 1986 levels starting in 1992.

The protocol has run into trouble in the undeveloped world from the beginning. Developing nations are generally less eager to comply than are the industrialized nations. CFCs are very

desirable and inexpensive and those nations, unlike the industrial ones, have not yet had the opportunity or the means or the technology to bend them to the use and benefit of their people and their economies. To a degree, they have therefore dragged their feet. Among the twenty-four nations that signed the treaty at its inception in September 1987, only eight were from the Third World. A year later eight more nations had ratified the treaty, but only two—Egypt and Mexico—were Third World nations. Yet the participation of the less-developed nations is indispensable if the CFC threat to the stratosphere is to be stopped. Without them the ozone layer cannot be protected.

Under the best scenario, consumption of the two most important CFCs covered by the treaty—CFC-11 and CFC-12— would fall by 15 to 35 percent by 1999. They would drop by 40 to 45 percent by 2009, which is the extended deadline for the developing nations to fall in line with the treaty (they were given an extra decade to cut their use of CFCs in half). If eight key Third World nations were not to participate—Brazil, China, India, Indonesia, Iran, Mexico, Saudi Arabia, South Korea— total global consumption of CFCs would drop by only 15 to 30 percent by 2009. This would fall far short of stopping the CFC threat in the stratosphere. By late 1988, just before the protocol took effect, only one of these critical eight nations had ratified the treaty—Mexico. By late 1989, the other seven still hadn't. Indonesia has signed the protocol, but not ratified it. Algeria, Iraq, South Africa, Taiwan, and Turkey all have been absent from discussions. Less than a score of Third World nations had signed the treaty by the end of 1989: Burkina Faso, Cameroon, Egypt, Ghana, Jordan, Kenya, Malaysia, Maldives, Malta, Mexico, Nigeria, Panama, Singapore, Thailand, Trinidad and Tobago, Tunisia, Uganda, and Venezuela.

If enough of the major Third World nations fail to participate, CFC consumption could actually increase despite the protocol. For the Third World will be the coming big user of CFC products—or their ozone-saving replacements. In China only one

household in ten now owns a refrigerator. And China's Communist leaders have vowed that there will be a refrigerator in every Chinese kitchen by 2000. If China is not participating in the protocol, and if the industrialized nations haven't helped it find a way to put those refrigerators in those kitchens without CFCs, it is going to add to the problem.

Moreover, the protocol, even under the most desirable of scenarios, with all the developing nations aboard and all of the reductions met, isn't going to be good enough. As unprecedented as the agreement is, as now written, it will not save the ozone layer. It has too many loopholes. The deadlines can't be met. And the threat to the ozone layer is far greater than the negotiators originally thought when they pounded out their hard-won agreement. More depletion of the ozone shield has occurred than they knew.

After the protocol was signed one of the two men who first sounded the ozone alarm nearly fifteen years earlier, F. Sherwood Rowland, said: "I think the situation is more dangerous than most of the nations are acknowledging. I'm sure there will be a call for more [reductions] as soon as the ink is dry on this treaty." That, of course, has happened.

The present protocol will not arrest depletion, but merely slow its momentum. That is not good enough. Besides, several chemicals not regulated under the treaty have now emerged as threats to the layer. Methyl chloroform and carbon tetrachloride are both miracle solvents. Together they contributed 13 percent of total ozone-depleting chemical emissions in 1985. They are not covered under the protocol. The U.S. Environmental Protection Agency says that 45 percent of projected chlorine growth in the stratosphere by 2075 will come from compounds still allowed under the treaty. Another 40 percent will come from compounds not covered, and 15 percent from nonparticipating nations. Rowland was right. The protocol was in a sense obsolete before it was signed. It clearly needed revision. And that is indeed happening. In late June 1990, parties to the protocol agreed to phase

out CFCs by 2000, strengthen its halon provisions, and bring the other ozone-depleting chemicals under protocol control.

Only the five CFCs considered most damaging to the ozone layer were banned in the original agreement—CFC-11 and CFC-12 (the refrigerants), CFC-113 (the cleaning agent), and CFC-114 and CFC-115 (variety of uses). But these are the superstars of the CFC industry. The first three constitute more than 90 percent of all CFCs made in the U.S. Substitutes for the ozone-puncturing CFCs may be within reach (no substitutes for halons, however, have yet been identified). Final decisions on types and costs await completion of toxicity tests by a consortium of producers. That will take two to four years. If the industry is to be believed, substitutes to the CFCs will be neither easy nor cheap. And there will be problems putting all of the research and development, redesign, and conversion together into a final package.

The auto and electronic industries expect to find the going hardest. Carmakers in the U.S. put thirty-thousand tons of CFC-12 annually in automobile air conditioners. The heir-apparent to CFC-12 in automobiles is a hydrofluorocarbon numbered HFC-134a. It is not a drop-in replacement. Automakers will have to develop new systems compatible with it, at a cost they put at hundreds of millions of dollars. Already crowded engine compartments will have to make room for bigger units, and such rearranging is never minor or inexpensive. The successors to the efficient CFCs, besides being more bulky, will also be more complex and less efficient.

The electronics industry, which relies on CFCs to clean its tiny and sensitive components, may be even harder pressed than the auto industry. It claims that there is still no really good replacement to the wonder compound it has grown to rely on—CFC-113. IBM alone uses nearly three-thousand tons of this chemical in its global operations. It is not proving easy to develop a substitute that will clean electronic components as thoroughly as CFC-113 does and still not damage them. The plastics industry,

which must also shift over if the limits of the Montreal Protocol are to be met, will find it easier than both the auto and electronics industries. It has adequate substitutes available now and they can be dropped in with a minimum of disruption.

Difficult or not, expensive or not, these conversions have got to be made. Mario Molina, one of the two discoverers of the trouble in the ozone layer, doubts that it will be as expensive as the industry insists. "In any case," he says, "the world cannot afford the consequences of continuing to release CFCs into the atmosphere."

Planting Trees, Hauling Wood, and Fixing Dunes

In Thailand, a young woman moves barefoot between the long rows of straight young trees. Across her shoulders a long wooden rod bends under the weight of two large watering cans suspended on either side. As she makes her way down the row, she tips first one of the big cans then the other. A spray of water cascades out, hits the new-turned ground and seeps in.

The young Thai is watering newly-planted seedlings. She can't save the environment alone doing this. But perhaps millions like her doing the same thing in India and Haiti and Brazil and Indonesia and Malaysia and Peru and every other nation of the world can. Reforesting the earth may be one of the planet's salvations in the coming century of crisis. And it is beginning to happen.

It has been happening for forty years in China, primarily out of pressing necessity. One billion people create an overwhelming demand for wood—to build with, cook with, heat with, and make paper with. All of this wood must come from within China itself, from its own forests, which are not all that plentiful. China has but 300 million acres of forestland, only one-tenth as much as we have in the United States, not a lot for a nation of such size.

So the Chinese have planted trees, millions of trees, nearly 75

million acres since 1949. Forest area in relation to total land area in China rose from 8.6 percent to 12.7 percent between 1949 and 1979. The goal is 20 percent by the end of this century. Another 340 million acres have been staked out as potential forest land. What China has done is impressive, beyond anything any other nation has done, the largest single example of successful reforestation in the world.

But there are others. In Gujarat State in India a forestry project was started in the 1970s. The goal was to distribute and plant 30 million seedlings a year. Farmers began to see that planting trees could be profitable; there was a strong demand for poles in India. So they began planting. Schoolchildren also began planting and starting up nurseries for seedlings. Within three years seedling distribution jumped from 17 million a year to nearly 200 million. By 1983 one in every ten of Gujarat's farmers had became involved. Ten trees were being planted each year for every person in the state. The equivalent of 370,000 acres was reforested.

In Uttar Pradesh, another Indian state, another social forestry project was started with a five-year goal of planting twenty thousand acres of woodlots and fifty-five thousand acres of strip plantations. The goal was exceeded within three years. Some thirty-two thousand acres of degraded forest were rehabilitated, and seventeen million workdays of employment were generated in the process, including four million days for women.

In Haiti in 1981 the Agency for International Development put up $8 million to promote tree planting as a cash crop for farmers. More than thirteen million seedlings have been planted. More than sixteen million, double the original goal, will have been planted by the time the project ends. It has involved thousands of farm families in Haiti, a country with the lowest annual per capita of gross national project and one of the highest ratios of people to arable land in the Western Hemisphere. Most farmers involved in the project have planted 200 to 250 trees a year apiece.

In Kenya, the greenbelt movement sponsored by the National Council of Women has mobilized more than fifteen thousand farmers and half a million schoolchildren to plant more than two million trees. Even in the industrial nations people are planting. The American Forestry Association has proposed an urban reforestation program to plant one hundred million trees in cities and suburbs around the U.S. by 1992.

Reforesting an area of the world the size of two Texases by the year 2000—the recommended goal—appears on the surface to be out of the question. But these examples from China, India, Haiti, Kenya, and the U.S. prove it may not be. It would require planting 18.4 billion trees a year—five seedlings for each person now living in the Third World. The pool of labor for planting on that scale—farmers, the jobless, women, schoolchildren—is enormous. It would be a project requiring extraordinary feats of organization. But a few individual nations are proving it is not impossible.

Moreover, good news has recently come from the research laboratory. Botanist A. F. Mascarenhas and two of his colleagues at the National Chemical Laboratory in Pune, India, have recently coaxed bamboo to flower in a laboratory setting. It is a feat never before managed. The new technique could allow botanists to breed a better version of bamboo faster than heretofore possible. Bamboo in the field can take more than a century to flower and produce seeds. This new development could be a quantum breakthrough for reforestation, "a breakthrough," says University of Cambridge botanist David Hanke, "that could have real significance for a quarter of the world's population."

Bamboo has underpinned the economies and cultures of Asia and many tropical nations for centuries. It has traditionally been a key source of lightweight, rot-resistant wood for homes and smaller public buildings. In the Third World, this useful grass is also a dietary staple for livestock. This new technique could dramatically quicken forestation in regions where stands of bamboo have been depleted or devastated.

Sandra Postel and Lori Heise, writing for the Worldwatch

Institute, have said: "Tree planting may lack the glory and grandeur of a medical breakthrough, a huge hydropower dam, or any number of technological marvels. But its unmatched potential for stabilizing simultaneously the carbon cycle, land and water resources, rural energy supplies, and people's livelihoods makes it a top priority for economic and social development."

By 1973 the typical South Korean housewife was having a problem. It was a simple, everyday problem that she seemed to share with one in every four housewives in the world. Fuelwood was getting hard to come by. And she depended heavily on fuelwood. It was what she cooked with and what she heated with. Around her village the forests that had always supplied her need were overcut and depleted.

The South Korean government couldn't help noticing the problem too, because soil was eroding and flooding was sweeping away slopes left bare around village after village. So, to the housewife's relief, the government launched a program. Its centerpiece was the fuelwood problem. The goal was to establish and intensively manage tree plantations to meet the fuelwood crisis. It was called the Village Fuelwood Program.

South Korea attacked across a broad front. Its villagers started planting trees. Within five years they had planted more than two and a half million acres of them, including six hundred thousand acres of woodlots in twenty thousand villages to take care of the fuelwood needs of housewives. One and a half million acres of existing fuelwood plantations and more than seven and a half million additional acres of forest land were brought under tighter management. More than three billion seedlings were produced and planted. Three-quarters of all forest land in South Korea is in private hands. So landowners were encouraged either to plant it themselves or give up nonagricultural land so somebody else could.

Funding for the reforestation drive came through a specially created Village Forestry Authority. The costs of seedlings and fertilizer were subsidized to encourage grassroots participation

at the village level. It worked. The participation came. The most appropriate tree species and planting techniques were marshalled. Because the program was efficiently managed, the financing, materials, and information the villagers needed was at hand when needed.

The government developed a more efficient system of underfloor heating that cut fuelwood consumption for warmth and cooking by 30 percent. It has caught on in the villages. Sale of fuelwood, particularly to city residents, was outlawed, reducing fuelwood demand at the local level and illegal cutting at the same time. The government also pushed rural electrification hard. And fuelwood consumption fell from 55 percent of total energy consumption in 1966 to 19 percent by 1979.

Not all of the more than three-score nations with major fuelwood shortages have handled it as well as the Koreans. But all of them know that dealing with the problem of forests in the Third World means dealing with the problem of fuelwood. It, and not electricity or coal or oil or natural gas, is the main source of domestic energy for half of humanity. Today nearly a billion people are hewing wood for their energy needs faster than it can grow back. In the rural Himalayas and sub-Saharan Africa, women and children now spend between one hundred and three hundred days a year simply scavenging firewood, primarily deadwood. They can spend a day collecting enough wood to last them for only three or four days.

Some one hundred million people in twenty-three countries can't find enough wood to meet their needs, even by overcutting the forests. Many of these are molding cakes of animal dung and burning it to bridge the gap. An estimated four hundred million tons of dung is burned for fuel every year, robbing croplands of nutrients and cutting food-grain harvests by more than fourteen million tons in the process.

A good two-thirds of the Third World—sixty-three of ninety-five nations—have a major fuelwood shortage. Half of the developing world could lack a sustainable supply by the year 2000. Over half of the countries most lacking in fuelwood are in sub-

Saharan Africa, for shortages are most acute in semiarid and mountain areas where natural woodlands are unproductive and the risk of overexploiting the environment is greatest. The inhabitants of more than a third of all the nations with fuelwood shortages have nowhere to go but to the figurative woodpile for energy. They either have no proven oil or gas reserves or they lack the economic means to switch from fuelwood to fossil fuels. They are in a dilemma—and the rest of the world with them: With either fuel they are hurting the environment.

For decades farmers and their sons and their sons after them have intensively cultivated the *niayes* in Senegal, the fertile enclaves of land by the coastal sand dunes between Dakar and St. Louis. For all those decades the grass cover and the acacia trees held back the desert and the gardens prospered. The *niayes* were the livelihood of thousands of Senegalese, producing tons of vegetable crops every year. The gardens were very productive. They earned the farmers good money. But, driven to make them even more productive and profitable, the farmers began clearing new fields. More people came in, swelling the population, collecting firewood, and grazing livestock. Soon a pattern very familiar to the Sahel began to emerge. The grass cover diminished, the acacias and the shrubs began to thin. Wind erosion picked up and the dunes began to march.

But there the old pattern took on a new twist. The Senegalese didn't retreat before the shifting sands. They stayed and fought back. In 1973 the government got United Nations financial help and began using the latest techniques in dune stabilization. Inland from the beach dunes, six thousand acres of acacias were planted in and around the farm fields to stem wind erosion, regenerate the fertility of the soil, and give livestock forage. Over six hundred kilometers of eucalyptus and cashew windbreaks were planted. The large stretch of coastal dunes were stabilized.

Even as the Senegalese were proving that it could be done, that the sand could be stopped and the land saved, a notable global

movement with a far greater reach was just getting underway. It has proved that land can also be saved on a planetary scale.

The International Union for Conservation of Nature and Natural Resources (IUCN) was commissioned in the late 1970s to map a strategy of conservation worldwide. Its brainchild was the World Conservation Strategy, launched in 1980. The WCS has the nations writing national strategies. Forty such strategies have either been written or are being developed. Indonesia, Malaysia, the Philippines, Thailand, Zambia, Nepal, Vietnam, Sri Lanka, and Uganda in the Third World have completed their strategies. In the industrialized world strategies or drafts are ready in Australia, South Africa, Spain, the United Kingdom, New Zealand, Italy, Canada, Norway, and the Netherlands. All of these strategies have three main things in common. All are written to maintain essential ecological processes and life-support systems such as soils and forests. All preserve the full array of biological diversity in their ecosystems and their species. And all ensure that these ecosystems and species are used by humans on a sustainable basis.

Meanwhile the IUCN has been working to preserve ecological systems worldwide. In consort with nations and groups of nations, these things have been done:

- Two hundred forty-four Biosphere Reserves have been set up in sixty-five countries, fifty-nine of them in twenty-nine tropical countries where the need is greatest.

- Fifty-seven World Heritage Sites have been set aside, twenty-five of them in equatorial countries.

- Three hundred and one wetland areas in thirty-seven countries have been protected, several of them adjacent to tropical forest ecosystems.

- Brazil, where the precious rain forest is disappearing so rapidly in the consuming thirst for cleared land, is attempting to develop an extensive system of protected areas. Some seven and a half million acres are targeted for protection when all

of its proposed Ecological Stations and reserves are established.

- Peru has set up a system of more than twenty parks and protected areas similar to Brazil's and covering more than ten million acres. Four of the largest of these are in the Amazon rain forest.

- Indonesia plans to place 15 percent of its land area under protection, more than five hundred conservation units in eight categories.

- India is setting aside thirteen Biosphere Reserves, representing nine of the twelve major biogeographic provinces in the nation. They will supplement India's forty-four national parks and its more than two hundred wildlife sanctuaries. The total conservation area is more than twenty million acres.

- The Soviet Union is also setting aside preserves. Gorbachev has announced that "there are ecosystems on the territory of this country that have not yet been affected by human activity. Therefore, we attach great importance to the creation of preserves and other protected territories. By 2000 their area is to increase approximately three times. These are unique nature laboratories situated over a vast territory from the Arctic islands to Central Asia."

These are all the work of nations. Private groups are also active, mainly in the industrial world. In the United States, the Nature Conservancy now manages more than 750 reserves.

These efforts to plant trees, solve the Third World's fuelwood problem, fix its invading sands, and preserve its precious ecosystems are not comprehensive. They will not of themselves save the environment. But they point up the possibilities. They tell me it is not too late to save ourselves. They tell me that there are people and nations in the world willing to unite against the four potential killers of our planet.

11

Legislating for a Safer Planet

Early in 1990, two significant environmental events occurred in Washington. In February, President Bush addressed the Intergovernmental Panel on Climate Change (IPCC). In April, the Senate passed the Clean Air Act.

Although it could have been otherwise, the two events demonstrated how difficult it will be for the human race to come together to combat the degradation of the world environment. I have already described the troubled passage of the clean air bill through the Senate.

Business as Usual

The president's address to the IPCC was deeply disappointing. It had been widely anticipated as an opportunity for him to educate Americans on the scope of the threat and to assert American leadership in a worldwide effort to deal with it. Instead, after much-publicized infighting within his administration over the tone and content of the speech, the president delivered a flat, narrow address which left his listeners unimpressed and his nation uninspired.

In his address the president announced a program of research to develop better models of world climate. He told of plans to expand and improve our system for monitoring atmospheric gases, temperatures, and other environmental effects.

Obviously, more research is warranted. The scientific community has done an excellent job of making us aware of the potential catastrophe that is stalking us. We have a basic obligation to learn about and understand all the implications as thoroughly and as quickly as science permits.

But the president did not seize the opportunity he had to act as well as to urge more study.

The arguments for business as usual won out over the arguments to begin now to do what we can to slow our contribution to the warming earth.

The arguments for business as usual are too familiar to need repeating. I can't count the number of times I have heard them. Unwarranted claims of enormous, unsustainable costs are raised against virtually every environmental initiative our government has ever tried to take. Exaggerated predictions of economic collapse are revived at every suggestion that our society change some of its ways. Partisan motives are ascribed to those who dare to suggest that the survival of a healthy environment represents a crucial public policy goal.

We heard those same arguments year after year in the acid rain debate. First there was a reluctance to believe in the phenomenon in the first place. Then there were pseudoscientific claims that acidification was a hitherto unknown but entirely natural phenomenon. Next there were the predictions of regional economic collapse. Finally there were calls for study, and more study, and extravagant disputes over relatively minor scientific uncertainties.

And for ten years the problem worsened. Streams and lakes suffered and, as I have described in this book, whole forests were affected. Finally, the need for action became so obvious that we had to act to control acid rain.

I recite this history because those who fail to remember the

past are doomed to relive it. I very much fear that we are at the threshold of yet another sterile, wasteful, and ultimately unnecessary debate over global warming.

Such a prolonged debate would be sterile, because there is no dispute that the concentration of greenhouse gases in our atmosphere has risen over the past century. There is no dispute that these gases trap heat near the earth's surface. And there is no dispute that heat at the earth's surface affects the earth's climate. It would be a wasteful debate because as long as policymakers are rehearsing old arguments, they are not acting; they are not taking the steps that must be taken. It would be a profoundly unnecessary debate because, at bottom, the steps we must take in response to global warming are the very same steps that we must take for sound environmental and economic reasons anyhow—right now.

Yet instead of pointing our society toward such a conserving and sensible approach, the president's seminal speech called for more study.

The best scientific information we have today is that the concentration of greenhouse gases already in the atmosphere—the relic of past fossil fuel consumed by our industries, our homes, and our automobiles—has committed us to an increase in the warming of the atmosphere, no matter what we do today.

The secretary-general of the World Meteorological Organization has said it as plainly as it can be said:

> The Global warming to which we are already committed is irreversible. . . . By the time we detect it, it will be too late.

It is true that we cannot predict specifically and with pinpoint certainty just how much of a temperature increase will occur by which decade of the next century. It is also true that we cannot predict specifically what such a comparatively sudden temperature rise will do to farmlands, to the air in our cities, or to the ocean currents that moderate coastal climates.

We can no more predict specific outcomes than the medical

community can predict which individuals will succumb to cancer. Climate change is much like tracking disease: We can see evidence that it exists and we can predict that it will occur. We can demonstrate the cause-and-effect cycle. We can construct statistical projections. But we cannot spell out precisely who will be affected and precisely how.

These are unanswerable questions, but they are as unanswerable by the proponents of business as usual as they are by those concerned about the answers. Neither side can say with certainty that one prediction is false or another is true. The things we do know with certainty are that the phenomenon has occurred, that the speed at which it has taken place is unprecedented in the experience of human existence on this planet, and that we cannot reverse its effects within a human lifetime.

When we are faced with a potential catastrophe whose precise timing and effect we cannot predict, the sensible and conserving response is to take preventive action. People in California cannot know when or how hard the next earthquake will hit. But that lack of specifics is no reason to abandon earthquake construction standards. But in a case where what is at stake is the future of our planet, we are told that the lack of specific data is a good enough reason to do as little as possible.

The president does not base his national security strategy on such a standard. He would be irresponsible if he did. It is past time that all of us accepted the environmental threat with the same seriousness we now automatically extend to the threat of a missile strike.

The president said that some may want to exploit the issue of global warming for political purposes. He accused some of wanting to abandon the free-market principles of prosperous economies. But these are red herrings and he knows they are red herrings.

Nobody suggests abandoning the free market. Nobody is advocating extreme measures. There is no huge politically motivated call for drastic revisions of our economy or our society. These

arguments are straw men, erected because they are so easy to demolish.

But discrediting exaggerated arguments is no answer to real ones. The real arguments are far more serious and demand a more serious response.

Greenhouse gases are being released into the atmosphere much faster than they are being removed. Even if we could hold emissions totally constant, the concentration of these gases would continue to intensify for the next century. If the majority of the scientific community is right, the level of carbon dioxide alone will nearly double from 1985 to 2010—from five billion tons to nine billion tons. The question is not *if* that will make the earth warmer; the question is when and by how much? As we have seen, carbon dioxide is only one of the threatening greenhouse gases. We know even less about some of the others.

Although our earth has known comparatively abrupt climate shifts before, never has the earth and all its life systems faced such a change so suddenly. Temperature rises which occurred over millennia—thousands of years—now threaten to occur within one hundred years. No wonder the scientific community cannot predict what the outcome will be with certainty.

But it is one thing to recognize uncertainty in specific predictions. It is another to suggest that because the specifics cannot be known, the larger claim is without foundation. It is even worse to do so when the steps that should be taken are steps that should be taken whether there is global warming or not.

The United States today uses two units of energy to produce one unit of output compared with the energy use of Japan or West Germany. Energy inputs are an industrial cost. Clearly, our competitive economic standing worldwide demands that we improve our energy efficiency. If for no other reason than to compete in world markets, we should be moving aggressively, now, to encourage energy conservation, energy efficiency, and non-fossil-fuel alternatives.

The president said we have to move "beyond the practice of

command, control, and compliance" to a "new kind of environmental cooperation."

I agree. We do. But words alone won't get us there.

It was the original clean air law, not hopeful words, which made the mileage of the U.S. auto fleet double between 1976 and 1986. It was the pressure of the oil embargo and conservation requirements in law that enabled American output to grow by 40 percent without an increase in energy use for thirteen years.

We have a textbook example of the difference between leadership and the lack of it in our own recent history. When oil prices fell in 1981 and President Reagan rejected conservation entirely, those advances stopped. We did not have "a new kind of environmental cooperation." We had business as usual. So oil imports are back up to 50 percent of our consumption. We remain vulnerable to price and supply disruptions today almost as though the disruptions following 1973 had never happened.

The president of the Electric Power Research Institute says that by the middle of the next century the generation of electricity by current methods could use as much energy as the entire world consumes for all purposes today. Clearly, our fossil-fuel heritage will not be equal to that demand. Alternative energy sources will be needed long before that point is reached if we intend to preserve decent living standards.

Conservation of existing fossil fuels, more efficient use of what fuels we do burn, protection of existing forests as well as reforestation, and new energy sources—all of these are steps we should take promptly for reasons of their own. Each has a logical, economically sound rationale. Yet the president spoke as though advocating such steps constitutes a radical program entirely at odds with the priorities of our nation and the needs of our natural environment.

On February 2, 1990, half of the Nobel Prize–winning scientists in our country and almost half of the members of the National Academy of Sciences wrote the president a letter, urging that he take immediate and practical policy steps to combat global

warming. These are among the most scientifically literate Americans living today.

Yet in his address the president spoke instead of the problem of "politics and opinion . . . outpacing the science." But his problem is the opposite: The science has far outpaced the politics and opinion which underlay his speech.

The two pioneering atmospheric chemists quoted earlier, Graedel and Crutzen, mentioned as particularly troubling the possibility of "unwelcome surprises." They cited in particular the shock waves that the discovery of the Antarctic ozone hole sent through the scientific community. But sometimes the surprises are the only things that will move us to act.

The ozone hole over the Antarctic was reported in 1985. Four years later, we joined an international agreement to reduce CFCs by half by the year 2000. The Clean Air Act revision calls for a total ban. Those comparatively swift steps were taken in response to projections of two million more skin cancer cases each year, damage to human constructions in the range of $2 billion per year, and incalculable damage to crops and aquatic life.

But scientists, led by Drs. Molina and Rowland, began warning us about these compounds in the mid-seventies. Then, however, as now with global warming, the proponents of business as usual prevailed. The major uses of CFCs remained in place, even as they were phased out of a handful of consumer products. Total worldwide production of CFCs rose 16 percent in just four years of the last decade. Then, finally, when the evidence of the ozone destruction was specific enough to suit the doubters, when the predictions of skin cancer could be quantified enough to yield numbers, agreement was reached to begin phasing them out. Perhaps this year the Congress will vote to ban the substances. CFCs will stay in the atmosphere for about a century, so ozone thinning will continue. And the price of doing business as usual will, as usual, be borne by our children.

What those distinguished scientists said about the ozone hole is just as true of climate change. Indeed, what is most disturbing

about the greenhouse effect is precisely the fact of uncertainty as to specifics, combined with clear evidence of massive factors at work. These factors call for a major effort to educate Americans to recognize that the greenhouse effect is not a pleasant hope for warmer spring weather in the next century, but a potentially cataclysmic danger to our world.

We will have to explain to a nation of city dwellers that our basic foodstuffs, the wheat for our bread and the grains that feed our livestock, have a very narrow tolerance for temperature swings. Corn yields are affected when rainfall drops below twenty inches a year and when summer temperatures rise too high.

We must make clear that even though we cannot precisely predict how much polar melting may occur or how high ocean levels may rise, that even a rise of a single foot—which is well within the expected range of ocean level increases—will erode many of our coastal beaches, contaminate the groundwater of our coastal communities with saltwater, and flood the wetlands that are the breeding grounds of some of our great fisheries.

We must convey to people that a minor change in temperature may mean a major change in national life.

We must do that responsibly. If we want the American people to understand the problem and to give long-term unwavering support for solutions, we will have to build a consensus on firm, clear knowledge, not on half-baked suppositions or scare tactics.

Unfortunately, the president's chief of staff chose to do the latter. He said, "I don't think America wants not to be able to use their automobiles." Nobody has suggested such a possibility. He referred to faceless bureaucrats trying to "cut off our use of coal, oil, and natural gas." The president spoke of the fact that legitimate concerns would be exploited by some. He should also have warned that entirely false concerns might well be raised by others.

The fact is that global warming is a problem that will demand the broadest, most thoroughly grounded public support if we are to respond effectively and preserve our living standards.

Thirty years ago Americans recognized the truth that our earth is shared in common by us all: We understood that we could no longer treat our waters and our atmosphere as a common dumping ground. Our nation has made enormous strides in cleaning up pollution since that time.

Today our challenge is to recognize that changes caused by the well-meaning efforts of human beings to live more comfortably and feed themselves better may be causing irreversible damage to the very earth in which all our hopes of nourishment and comfort are grounded.

I have described in Chapter 1 the hard, rocky road to cleaner air. The way has proved difficult on another legislative front as well.

Wetlands Protection: A Good Thing Gone Wrong

Ten days before Thanksgiving in 1989 President Bush signed the North American Wetlands Conservation Act into law. It was in itself a day of thanksgiving. I was pleased and proud to have conceived the law and been its author. It was designed to arrest and reverse the dramatic decline of wetlands on our continent. It initiated a major new public and private effort to conserve these precious and fragile lands and the migratory birds and other fish and wildlife that depend on them.

A principal goal of the legislation is to begin a long-term U.S. commitment to implement the North American Waterfowl Management Plan. This 1986 bilateral agreement between the U.S. and Canada seeks to restore the continent's waterfowl numbers by conserving nearly two million acres of wetland ecosystems in the U.S. and about four million acres in Canada.

As chairman of the Senate Subcommittee on Environmental Protection during 1987 and 1988, I found that the North American Waterfowl Management Plan failed to back its ambitious goals with any commitment for funding or even to lay out a strategy for its implementation. Consequently there has been

relatively little progress in reaching its goals over the past three years. The North American Wetlands Conservation Act was intended to correct these shortcomings in the plan and in its implementation.

The act directs the secretary of the interior to match federally-appropriated funds with nonfederal funds to protect, restore, and enhance wetlands in the U.S., Canada, and Mexico. Wetlands conservation projects are to be identified and recommended by a nine-member North American Wetlands Conservation Council made up of representatives from the U.S. Fish and Wildlife Service, state fish and wildlife agencies, and charitable nonprofit conservation organizations such as the Nature Conservancy and Ducks Unlimited. The final decision on project funding will be made by the existing Migratory Bird Conservation Commission, which consists of the secretaries of the interior and agriculture, the EPA administrator, and two members each from the House and the Senate.

The act earmarks $25 million annually in federal matching funds to encourage the public and private partnerships needed for federal acquisition of wetlands, purchase of perpetual easements, and restoration and enhancement of wetlands. Federal funds also may be conveyed to states or private organizations for these purposes. Between 50 percent and 70 percent of the federal matching funds available each year must be spent on wetlands conservation projects in Canada and Mexico.

Funding for the program will come primarily from interest earned on receipts from the 10 percent federal excise tax on arms and ammunition and from fines under the Migratory Bird Treaty Act.

Finally, the act requires the secretary of the interior to work with the appropriate officials of other nations in the Western Hemisphere to establish additional agreements to protect migratory bird habitat.

It was my hope that the act would reverse the steady decline of wetlands that has taken place since Europeans first came to

the North American continent. That will be extremely difficult in the face of rising population and development pressures. But it must be done.

While I was heartened by the president's words of support for wetlands preservation, I was dismayed when shortly after signing the act into law, the administration did two things that contradict the spirit and intent of the act.

On December 1, 1989, the director of the U.S. Fish and Wildlife Service sent to the service's regional offices a bold action plan entitled, "Wetlands: Meeting the President's Challenge." The director had apparently read, believed, and acted on the president's public statements on the need to preserve wetlands. Soon thereafter, unfortunately, the director was ordered by his superiors in the Interior Department to withdraw his action plan. As of this writing, no further word has been heard on how the department intends to apply the law.

In another unfortunate and untimely step backward on November 14, the day after the president signed the act, the administration suspended implementation of a Memorandum of Agreement between the Army Corps of Engineers and the EPA. The agreement resolved a long-standing dispute between the corps and the EPA over the administration of those provisions of the Clean Water Act relating to wetlands. The administration's suspension of its implementation was again inconsistent with the president's public statements on wetland policy.

A revised version of the agreement was signed on February 6, 1990. It spelled out the policy and procedures that will govern the type and level of mitigation necessary to comply with the environmental requirements for filling wetlands under Section 404 of the Clean Water Act.

The continued reluctance of the administration to put this limited wetlands protection agreement into effect raised serious doubts about the level of commitment to the president's oft-stated goal of no net loss of wetlands. And now this revised wetlands accord reflects the price paid by the EPA and the army

for the administration's acquiescence to its implementation. It may prove too high a price. The changes made to the original agreement not only threaten to undo the agreement itself, they threaten to undermine the EPA's environmental regulations for Section 404 wetland filling permits.

Two key changes were made in the original agreement that thwart its intent to ensure that, to the extent practicable, damage to wetlands is minimized and what damage remains is offset.

First, the revised agreement allows deviation from the stepwise consideration of avoidance, minimization, and compensation for what are termed "insignificant environmental losses." The original accord allowed deviation from this sequence only when "the EPA and the Corps agree that the proposed discharge can reasonably be expected to result in environmental gain." The administration-imposed revision adds the phrase "or insignificant environmental losses" to the end of this sentence.

If insignificant environmental losses are not clearly confined to de minimus discharges or discharges that do only minimal individual and *cumulative* environmental damage, this change could permit wetlands to be lost that otherwise might be saved. Moreover, the term "insignificant environmental losses" is not defined or clarified by the agreement and it is not a term used in the Clean Water Act or the Section 404 regulations. Therefore, it is likely to generate many disputes between developers and regulators over whether proposed discharges into wetlands are environmentally damaging.

The second and more egregious change on which the administration insisted could seriously undercut and weaken the present EPA environmental guidelines for filling in areas where there is a high proportion of wetlands. The revised accord adds a footnote that ostensibly seeks to clarify that it may not always be practicable to mitigate the extent needed to ensure no net loss of wetland values. The footnote says that "avoidance, minimization, and compensatory mitigation may not be practicable where there is a high proportion of land which is wetlands."

The potential scope of this possible exception to stepwise consideration of measures to avoid, minimize, and offset wetland damage is enormous. Most important wetland areas of the United States may qualify as "areas where there is a high proportion of land which is wetlands," because the geographic frame of reference for the phrase is not clear.

For instance, does this phrase encompass all of the nation's coastal areas? Does it refer to any county or city with a high proportion of wetlands? Moreover, the agreement does not clarify what proportion of land has to be wetlands for it to qualify as "high."

The current EPA environmental guidelines require all requests for wetland filling to meet the same standards of avoidance, minimization, and compensation regardless of whether they are in areas where there is a high or a low proportion of wetlands. These guidelines and the original agreement make clear that avoidance, minimization, and compensation are required only to the extent practicable. Practicability has nothing to do with the proportion of land that is wetlands.

By concluding in advance that avoidance, minimization, and compensation may not be practicable in areas where there is a high proportion of land that is wetlands, the revised agreement makes it far less likely that wetland damage will be avoided and that unavoidable damage will be minimized in such areas.

These administration-imposed changes in last November's agreement, which began on such a promising note, call into serious question whether additional protection of wetlands in their natural state will be encouraged at all. It may now be difficult if not impossible to prevent the net loss of these valuable aquatic resources.

The wetlands agreement certainly does not match the president's rhetoric in support of a national goal of no net loss of wetlands. It is only one more example of the president's environmental deeds being inconsistent with his high-sounding environmental words. I only hope that the corps and the EPA will

interpret their revised policy guidance in a manner that preserves the integrity of the Clean Water Act's environmental standards for wetlands filling. It may be the only hope we have left.

State Action: The Tail That Wags the Dog

Alarm over what unbridled climate change might do to them and their economies has stirred a flurry of legislation in the states. The results have often been mixed. But just as often their legislation has been more farsighted and considerably ahead of federal action.

In the decade between 1976 and 1986, forty-two states reduced their emissions from oil burning; but forty-two states in that decade increased their coal burning emissions. From 1980 to 1985, American coal production rose from 830 million tons to 881 million. But as it was rising, it was also changing. In 1980, western states were mining 251 million tons of a generally lower-sulfur-content, hence cleaner, coal. By 1985 they were mining 316 million tons. Meanwhile coal production in the high-sulfur coal mines of Appalachia and the Midwest was falling from 579 million tons to 565 million. The western coal producing states, therefore, not only accounted for the entire 51 million tons of total increased output in the United States, they also offset a 14 million ton decline in production in the eastern and midwestern states.

The rise of western coal is most dramatically seen in two states—Montana and Wyoming. In 1970 both states together produced 10.6 million tons. Five years later their production had quadrupled to 45.9 million tons. By the end of that decade, it had more than doubled again, to 104.3 million tons. Since then increases have not been as dramatic, but they have been steady.

Today eighty million Americans in thirty states live in areas that exceed ozone pollution limits. Fifteen states offer alternative energy tax credits to encourage use of nonfossil fuels. Sixteen fund ride-sharing programs to cut down gas consumption. Four New England states—Maine, Vermont, Massachusetts, and

Rhode Island—currently ban or restrict the purchase of CFC-generating styrofoam products. Five states—New York, Massachusetts, Wisconsin, New Hampshire, and Minnesota—have acid rain control programs; but the heaviest acid rain producing states have yet to act.

Oregon, ever an environmental leader, was the first state to ban the sale of CFCs in aerosol sprays. That was in June 1975, only a year after Molina and Rowland began warning the world about the CFC threat to the ozone layer. Oregonians did not wait for the conclusive evidence the CFC producers demanded. New York followed Oregon later that same year with a law requiring a label on aerosol spray cans, similar to the one on cigarette packs, to the effect that their use could harm the environment. New York also empowered its State Environmental Conservation Commission to ban the sale of aerosol cans if they did turn out to be as harmful as Molina and Rowland said they were. Massachusetts was the first state ever to file a lawsuit to stop the excessive emissions of CFCs.

Texas, one of the biggest states, leads them all in CO_2 emissions, putting out over 150 million tons a year. Vermont, one of the smallest, is the least contributor with but 1.3 million tons. The kind of fossil-fuel consumption the various states excel in varies according to their specialties. Seventy-seven percent of all carbon emissions in West Virginia come from coal; it is one of the nation's preeminent coal-mining states. Even so, West Virginia is not first in coal carbon emissions; Pennsylvania, Indiana, Texas, and Ohio are all ahead of it. West Virginia, however, does lead the nation in tons of CO_2 that it generates per million dollars in Gross State Product (the total value of goods and services it produces); it has an economy geared to carbon. Natural gas accounts for over 40 percent of all emissions in Louisiana, a natural gas state. The bigger states lead in oil-burning emissions of CO_2. Texas, understandably, is number one with 78 million tons; California is second with 61 million. Oil combustion accounts for 99 percent of all of Hawaii's emissions.

Some 130 climate change bills were introduced in twenty-two

state legislatures in 1989, the biggest barrage of such legislation ever. State activity has become what one observer has called "a sleeper of a trend. States may zip past the federal government when they're not looking." California, which has traditionally led the way in air pollution legislation, led all states in 1989 with 22 climate change measures. Hawaii had 18; Connecticut, 14; Illinois, 12; Massachusetts, 9; New York, 8; Missouri, 5; and Minnesota, 4.

Seven of the 130 bills introduced were passed in the first half of 1989, all of them dealing with CFC emissions. Vermont banned the sale or registration of cars with air conditioners using CFCs, beginning with the 1991 model year. Hawaii outlawed over-the-counter sale of CFC refrigerants, tightened repair standards, and promoted CFC recovery and recycling. Maine outlawed the use of CFCs in all plastic foam boards. Connecticut now requires its commissioner of environmental pollution to consider CFCs when developing the state's new municipal solid waste recycling program. Missouri mandated new procurement practices to reduce and eliminate state purchases of CFC-containing polystyrene foam, and banned the sale of products made or packaged in such materials. Montana now requires users of twenty gallons or more of halogenated solvents for commercial purposes to register them. Oregon, in the last half of 1989, passed a law directing the State Energy Office to draw up an energy plan to cut its greenhouse emissions by 20 percent by 2005.

Waiting on state legislative dockets in 1989 were surcharges on registrations and transfers of motor vehicles emitting CFCs; funding for reforestation; bills to research global warming; disposal fees for CFC-bearing appliances; taxes on "gas-guzzler" cars; funding for an international conference on global warming; studies of the impact of global warming—especailly rising sea levels—on state environments and economies; bills to separate CFCs from other waste; legislation to develop strategies to reduce emissions causing global warming; and even a bill calling on President Bush to hold a global environmental conference on the greenhouse effect.

One U.S. city, Irvine, California, has even passed an ordinance banning the use of all CFCs within the city limits beginning in July 1990. Other cities may follow suit.

This legislation on state and local levels indicates that there is a stirring in the land. Many Americans see the danger to the world environment and want to do something about it. But they must have a national government driven by the same urgency, a government willing to lead both them and the world. They don't have that now.

12

Why We Must Lead

For three-quarters of its more than two centuries as a nation—through the industrial and the chemical revolutions—the United States has been a major part of the problem.

We are today among the world's leading polluters. We emit a quarter of all carbon dioxides into the earth's atmosphere, well over a billion tons a year, five tons for every U.S. citizen and nearly five times the world per capita average. All of the deforestation in South America each year causes only half the increase in CO_2 in the atmosphere that we Americans do by other means. Our electric power plants account for a third of our carbon contribution. Nearly 85 percent of that one-third originates with our nearly thirteen hundred coal-fired generating plants; and nearly fifty more such air-polluting plants are on power company drawing boards. Our transportation, our 137 million cars and trucks getting twenty miles to a gallon of gas, contribute another third of our CO_2. The average American automobile driven ten thousand miles a year will release its own weight in carbon to the atmosphere—between one and two tons, more than the average world citizen generates in all of his activities combined. U.S. industry contributes another one-quarter of all our CO_2 emissions. Our buildings account for 12 percent.

193

We also generate 25 percent of the planet's nitrogen oxides, 15 percent of its sulfur dioxides, and 30 percent of its CFCs. The U.S. alone has nearly one hundred million household refrigerators and eighty million auto air conditioners that use CFCs. Therefore, we also lead the world in the use of these ozone-shredding chemicals. Every American uses over two and a half pounds of CFCs every year—six times the global average. Together with the USSR, we produce 45 percent of the world's greenhouse gases. In line behind these two front-runners, in descending order of their contribution of CO_2 to the atmosphere, are Western Europe and China. We are, with the world's two largest Communist nations, the Soviet Union and China, one of the three biggest coal-burning nations in the world. Pollution not only knows no national boundaries, it also pays no heed to ideology.

Although we are but 5 percent of the world's population, we consume a quarter of the planet's energy year in and year out; we are one of its leading energy wasters. We consume energy very inefficiently. Japan's and West Germany's economies both produce twice as much gross national product per unit of energy as ours does.

That long statistical indictment should be argument enough. We have a clear moral obligation to lead the world in undoing the damage we have done. But aside from that, we must lead because we can lead. No other nation has shown a stronger commitment—in money and in know-how—to cleaning up its own environment. And no nation possesses in greater abundance the intellectual and technological resources necessary to the international challenge. We are in a unique position to lead the attack. We have shown in crisis after national crisis, down through the years, that government, business, science, and the American public can unite in a common cause to anticipate and prevent disaster. The need to do that is as urgent now, in this crisis, as it has ever been in our history.

If the United States doesn't seize the moment and take the lead in this essential global crusade, if it doesn't find ways to scale

down its hemorrhage of greenhouse emissions, then what nation on earth will possibly have the initiative, the will, or the justification to scale back on its own? The answer is obvious. Few will. We cannot urge upon others what we will not do ourselves.

The time is long past when we can wait for others to lead. As William Ruckelshaus has said, "America's predominant place in the world requires that we act first on many questions. We can no longer depend on having the benefit of watching other Western democracies, then incorporating their experiences into our own."

It is now time for us to divert some of the technology that has made us the world's industrial pacemaker, and to use it to help save the world from self-destruction. We must now become part of the solution. We simply have too much to lose not to lead this global effort. We could give no greater gift to ourselves and to all nations.

The trio of energy policy thinkers from the Office of Technology Assessment, whom I quoted from liberally in an earlier chapter, make sense when they say that "the fact that one country acting alone cannot 'cure' global problems compounds the political burden." And they add:

> Yet the sheer magnitude of U.S. energy consumption indicates that the U.S. could have a significant impact on global carbon emissions by instituting savings within the cost-effective ranges established by existing technology. And the U.S., because of its energy-intensive past and present and its great technological ingenuity and capability, can be charged with great responsibility in effecting the transition to an era beyond fossil fuels. To do so, it must increase its own efficiency, develop a new array of energy sources and expand the energy possibilities for other countries.

They suggest that the U.S. might consider a twofold goal: First, increase the fraction of useful energy produced from nonfossil resources (by fuel substitution and more efficient combustion) by 20 percent by the end of this century. Second, increase

the output of goods and services per unit of energy consumed by at least 2.5 percent a year for at least two decades. Such goals, the trio suggests, "are challenging but achievable and could be a useful focus for the U.S. to assume leadership on this truly global issue."

President Bush has said that the U.S. "looks forward to playing a significant role in efforts to assess and respond to global climate changes." So far, as I have indicated earlier, there have not been deeds to match those words.

The record of the Reagan administration, as I have also indicated, was dismal. In those years not only did the United States not lead, except in the case of the Montreal Protocol, but President Reagan refused too many times even to cooperate. When more than a score of nations signed a protocol to reduce sulfur emissions and stem the spread of acid rain, the U.S. wouldn't sign. When a dozen nations agreed to reduce their output of nitrogen oxides by 30 percent over the next decade, the U.S. refused to join them. When Canada and Norway endorsed a world target of cutting CO_2 emissions by 20 percent by 2005, the U.S. committed to nothing. The Reagan administration withdrew U.S. funding support for the UN's family planning effort, a key element in lowering world fertility rates, just as many nations were rallying to its support.

During those eight years, when I was trying to get acid rain legislation enacted, I heard over and over again from the president and members of his administration that there ought not be any action taken because "We need to study more. We need to study more." What we needed was to act then, and we need to act now. One of our most glaring national lapses has been our past failure to listen and respond to the acid rain problem, because it acts in such invisible ways. For ten years the signals have been flashing. For ten years they have mainly been ignored. The record of the next four years and the years beyond must not be more of the same.

On the credit side of the ledger, George Bush, in the first year of his presidency, called for a ten-million-ton reduction of sulfur dioxide and a two-million-ton reduction of nitrogen oxide emissions in the U.S. in the next decade. This will amount to slightly less than a 50 percent reduction. But I welcome it. The president has also proposed an alternative fuels program, tighter tail-pipe emissions standards, and controls to reduce toxic air emissions by 75 percent within the next decade.

But the president has still failed to seize the moment internationally. We were a leader in shaping the Montreal Protocol. But we have precious little else to show by way of vigorous world leadership.

We can take justifiable pride in what we have done for the past two decades to roll back pollution of our own air and water. We have spent generously—billions of dollars over the past two decades—fighting pollution in our own country. We have spent $200 billion on air-pollution control alone, and more billions to clean up our polluted waterways and hazardous wastes and to preserve our parks and wildernesses. We have passed landmark legislation—the Clean Water Act, the Clean Air Act, the toxic waste cleanup fund, the Endangered Species Act, and a host of other laws. These actions, not always easily taken, nonetheless constitute a laudable national commitment to a cleaner and safer environment.

But that effort pales beside the coming global struggle. In that arena we continue to miss opportunities to do what is right. The coming challenge, as the facts make clear, will be beyond the power and resources of any one nation. It is clear to me that only a broad international effort can deal effectively with it. It is also clear to me that the United States holds the key.

But a much more intensive commitment and a much greater effort are now necessary. As Lincoln told the Congress 138 years ago, "we must think anew and act anew." Then perhaps we can save the planet.

13

What the U.S. Must Do

Any action against global climate change must begin with a call to arms. The problem must be moved to center stage of national and international consideration. It must begin to dominate our scientific, political, and diplomatic agendas, for it is that important. All of our skills and technologies must be mobilized at the highest levels. Then the problem must be given systematic attention. As one scientist has put it, "We've got to get the planet into intensive care."

And as William Ruckelshaus has said:

We need to face up to the fact that something enormous may be happening to our world. Our species may be pushing up against some immovable limits on the combustion of fossil fuels and damage to the ecosystems. We must at least consider the possibility that, besides those modest adjustments for the sake of prudence, we may have to prepare for far more dramatic changes, changes that will begin to shape a sustainable world economy and society.

I believe that immediately the United States must take these important preliminary steps:

199

- We must reinforce our role in the international and environmental organizations dedicated to saving the planet from terminal pollution. We must participate and we must lead. We must actively swing our support behind two major global goals: reducing CO_2 emissions by 20 percent by 2005 and reducing world population growth rates by half by the turn of the century. We have to help make both things happen. Eventually, we must ourselves reduce consumption of fossil fuels by 50 percent or more and we must persuade other nations to join us in that effort.

- We must elevate the problem of global climate change to the top level of consideration in the executive department. There should be an interagency committee on global environmental change in the White House and a Secretary of the Environment with a cabinet-level department to head it. And then the president must heed its advice, not ignore it. The existing mechanisms are inadequate. The scientific and policy implications of global climate change are simply too complex and too important not to be brought to the head of the table.

- We must bend all possible U.S. talent and technical expertise to the environmental wars—"get the best people together, identify the problems, brainstorm a research program, and fund it," as Wallace Broecker has put it. He believes, and I agree with him, that "over the next decade or so, we must ramp up our efforts by tenfold. The task is every bit as complex as the crusade to prevent cancer and the crusade to defend against nuclear missiles." And in our ramping up we must take care that our talent and know-how are made available to the Third World.

- We must immediately act on the national level, as many states have already done, to ban totally the use of CFCs.

Those are steps we must and can take now. In three other important areas the U.S. must also act: We must at long last create a new national energy strategy, we must launch a pervasive

reuse and recycling program, and we must reduce even more drastically our motor vehicle emissions.

Toward a National Energy Policy

Energy is the lifeblood of every modern society, especially American society. The freezing and the cooking of food, the heating and cooling of homes and buildings, the powering of cars, airplanes, and industries—no aspect of life in a modern nation is untouched by the need for and consumption of energy.

Because of this driving need, world energy consumption has grown fifteenfold since 1900. Most of this growth has been in the form of fossil fuels. Oil, coal, and natural gas are the primary sources, generating 78 percent of all global energy; renewables are estimated at 17 percent by the Worldwatch Institute, and nuclear power at 5 percent.

Energy consumption by a nation is obviously related to its industrial development. Thus, the United States, with the world's largest and most developed economy, is by far its greatest consumer of energy. We have pursued a cheap, fossil-fuel-based energy policy for so long, hiding the true costs of the energy consumed, that it will be difficult for us to devise and implement a sound national energy policy. But we must do so, for we have no other choice.

It should include these elements:

Better energy efficiency. Our technological ingenuity can, if properly focused, help us reduce the amount of energy we use for virtually every purpose. Examples are many, but among the more obvious: We can increase the fuel economy in our motor vehicles; we can insulate our buildings, our residences and our businesses, more efficiently; we can light our commercial buildings more efficiently; and we can install more effective equipment for generating our electricity.

All these improvements are feasible now, at no cost in

productivity—indeed, with improved productivity in some cases. All that is lacking is political will, of both the public and its leaders. Somehow that will must be summoned.

Conservation. The most efficient appliances will still waste energy unless used with care. Through most of our recent history our energy ethic has been one of waste. It must be changed to an ethic of conservation. Given the power of modern means of communication and the ability of the president to dominate those means, this is uniquely a presidential task. Ronald Reagan's laughing at conservation efforts was no laughing matter. It was dead serious and deadly wrong.

Natural gas. It is by far the most noble of the fossil fuels. It is efficient, cleaner burning, and can be used to heat homes, generate electricity, power industries, and transport people. Existing reserves of conventional sources of natural gas may last up to half a century; and as the cost of competing energy sources rise, nonconventional sources may become cost-effective. It must be used more widely and more wisely.

Coal. The good news is that there's a lot of it. The bad news is that it's a dirty fuel. Extracting it is difficult and dangerous. It's rough on the miners and on the environment. But its sheer quantity (at current production rates existing world reserves would last nearly three centuries) makes it imperative that we improve technologies to burn it more efficiently and cleanly. If we could make an atomic bomb we should be able to devise a way to burn coal cleanly.

By doing so we would not only be contributing to a cleaner America; we would also be helping attain a cleaner world. The reason can be summed up in one word: China. China has a lot of people (now more than a billion, soon to be a billion and a half) and a lot of coal, so much that it gets 80 percent of its total commercial energy from that source. That compares with an

average of 25 percent for other industrialized countries. If China continues to exploit its coal resources with minimal regard for the environment (and it shows every indication of doing so) efforts elsewhere will be overwhelmed by Chinese emissions. A universally available, truly clean coal technology would be of great benefit.

Solar power. In the year 1990, human beings consumed a quantity of fossil fuels equal to that which it took nature a million years to create. Obviously, at such rates of consumption year after year, it will eventually all be used up. Sooner or later there won't be any left. What will we do then? The answer is as obvious as the sun at noon on a clear July day. Solar power will eventually replace fossil fuels, as thoroughly as petroleum replaced whale oil as a lubricant and as fuel for lamps more than a century ago. Already, photovoltaic cells generate the electricity to power satellites and small calculators. A truly focused national effort could significantly accelerate the date on which solar power becomes commercially competitive. Its potential for preserving the world environment is enormous.

Other renewables. Wind power, geothermal, biomass, and solar thermal energies also have major roles to play in our environmental future. They are already competing in the market and may be closer to helping displace fossil fuels than we generally give them credit for. We should continue to push their development.

Energy efficiency, conservation, natural gas, solar power, other renewables, and clean coal. Taken together, as parts of a sensible, phased-in, and properly funded plan, they could form the basis for a first ever, commonsense and effective energy policy for our country.

We must, however, be wary of nuclear power. It may appear on the surface to be an attractive member of any alternative fuel

repertoire. But it isn't as it now stands. It has too many serious problems. Technologically, economically, and politically it is a pariah, given to Three Mile Island– and Chernobyl-sized accidents, accidents capable in their own right of poisoning the planet. If nuclear plants replaced all coal-fired power plants in the world, global warming could be cut by 20 to 30 percent by the middle of the next century. But it would require bringing a nuclear power plant on line somewhere in the world every one to three days for the next forty years. The cost would be $9 trillion; the pace of construction would be ten times larger than any the world has ever seen. Both figures are unthinkable. A totally safe reactor, a totally safe place to dispose of its deadly wastes, and a totally safe way to keep the wrong kind of nuclear materials from falling into the wrong hands—none of these things have been resolved. All are simply too far down the road technologically and politically. By the time they are resolved, if they ever can be, it will be too late. The projected global warming will be full upon us.

The repertoire of safer renewable energy sources, with the exception of fusion, are as close technologically, and they are instantly acceptable politically.

Biomass, consisting of wood and organic waste, already generates energy for much of the planet—an estimated 11 percent of world energy use. Its conversion to methane or alcohol fuels for transportation is a present possibility. Power plants fueled by urban solid waste may also become a modest economical source of energy as garbage disposal problems become increasingly acute. A method to separate combustible from noncombustible materials and devices to control emissions must still be perfected.

Wind power is another possible alternative source of energy with promise. But it still lacks a system that permits it to operate reliably at variable rotor speeds. Yet two billion kilowatt hours of wind-generated electricity were produced and sold in California in 1989.

Geothermal energy—extracting heat from underground masses of hot water or, in the future, hot rock—and ocean ther-

mal energy, which exploits the temperature difference between the ocean's warm surface waters and its cold depths, are also future possibilities for some regions of the world. They now have only limited applications. Yet geothermal energy now costs only six cents a kilowatt hour in some sites.

Solar thermal energy is already on line in California—280 megawatts now in use, with another 380 megawatts on order by utilities. The newest plant produces power at eight cents per kilowatt hour.

Another source of energy, older than the environmental crisis itself, is hydroelectric power. But the huge dams of the past are exorbitantly expensive. And they are hard on the environment in their own way, inundating farmlands and dislocating people. However hydroelectric power on a small scale may still prove a useful energy source for many countries.

Using It Again—and Again

We must use our resources much more efficiently. That means that we must first try simply to use less energy, and thereby reduce waste. Next in order, we must try to reuse things, then recycle them. Only as a last resort should they be burned or buried. It's a hierarchy of actions worth trying to live by.

To do that requires that these alternatives be considered in funding proposals. If the alternative is a capital-intensive incinerator, then recycling may be more economically attractive. The cost-avoidance value of trash, in short, is generally higher than the direct value of the trash in the secondary market, but that is still a cost that has to be figured in.

Secondary markets need to be stabilized. In some instances cities could pay to have paper picked up and still come out ahead of the alternative costs. In other instances—New Jersey is an example—a state surtax on landfill use is rebated to cities based on their tonnage of materials. There are obviously many ways this can be adjusted to suit local conditions. In the Netherlands,

the government maintains stockpiles of trash and sets price supports for it, so that when secondary market prices rise above the price support level, the government sells its stockpiles. It operates like an agricultural price support system.

The Netherlands now recycles more than half of its glass, paper, and aluminum. The potential savings are substantial: If half of the paper in the world were reused, almost twenty million acres of forest could be saved. Paper mills which use only recycled paper use only half the water for processing and cost less to build than those which use virgin pulp.

Each aluminum can that is recycled saves the equivalent of half a gallon of petroleum, and requires 5 percent of the energy that would be needed to extract the original material.

Rubber can be reused in road surfacing. It is otherwise difficult to get rid of; tire dumps are a national eyesore, and burning it, as anybody with a sense of smell knows, is out of the question.

Reusing plastics is difficult—for two reasons: There is not yet any way to separate out different kinds of resins for reuse, and plastics that use chlorine in their manufacture give off dioxins in the recycling process. However, the potential is there. Plastics can potentially replace lumber now used in fencing, pier supports, and like products. These new uses are now under development. They are already being given high priority in Japan because of the high cost of lumber there.

Recycling in the U.S. has now become an urgent matter. Efforts have escalated because our landfills are overflowing. We are exceeding capacity everywhere. About half of the country's cities will fill their landfills by the early 1990s. The costs of disposal rise $.50 to $1.00 per ton per mile as they are trucked farther away. For many communities, waste disposal strategies are no longer the money-making schemes they were in past decades. They have instead become strategies aimed at holding down costs.

Reuse and recycling by consumers in this country are only in

their infancy, but we are learning fast. Several cities and states are moving into recycling in a big way. Portland, Oregon, now recycles 22 percent of its municipal wastes. Smaller cities and states in general are moving faster because the alternative disposal costs are more onerous for them.

Other strategies are also feasible. Nine U.S. states have gone back to returnable bottles. Norway and Denmark, faced with a surfeit of plastic products, have limited the kinds of bottles and jars that can be used for packaging to about twenty. This means that they can be interchangeably reused for products such as mustard, ketchup, or soft drinks, without perceptible damage to consumer choice or market efficiencies. Marketing focuses on the labeling and the product rather than on the cuteness of the container.

Since packaging materials constitute 30 percent by weight and 50 percent by volume of all household trash in the U.S., this kind of approach may make economic sense. Clearly the economics of trash are changing. Auto catalytic converters, for instance, are being scavenged now by a Japanese firm in the U.S. One of every four tons of general cargo shipped from New York is now fiber—mostly paper—being sold to East Asian countries for whom the cost of used materials is lower than the cost of new materials.

Prices of virgin products and reused products should be leveled by eliminating or curtailing subsidies for raw materials that give them an artificial price advantage. Below-market timber selling is an example. Likewise, water costs, where water is a major production factor, should not be artificially cheap.

The federal Resource Conservation and Recovery Act of 1976 (RCRA) was in part designed to encourage recycling. But it has not been aggressively enforced. One of its provisions was intended to encourage every level of government to purchase recycled items as a priority. But by 1986, ten years after passage, the regulatory guidelines for only one product—fly ash in cement—had been promulgated.

All levels of government in the U.S. employ sixteen million persons and spend the equivalent of about one-third of the gross national product. There is a potentially enormous market there to encourage recycling of all kinds across the board, from rubber for road building to paper for tax forms to re-refined oil for government motor vehicles. Government is also a rich market for such potential products as low-cost insulation made from waste paper.

Despite the desirability of reducing waste, reusing it, or recycling it as a first priority, 90 percent of U.S. waste is still buried. The idea of transforming the waste into energy hasn't caught hold in any significant way. There are about 62 waste-to-energy plants operating in the U.S. today; 26 or so are under construction and 39 are in advanced planning. A 1978 law requires local utilities to purchase power produced by such facilities. So we are beginning to move in that direction. Incineration overseas has advanced far more rapidly than here: There are 350 waste-to-energy incinerators worldwide, half in western Europe. Since 1960, Japan has increased the capacity of its incinerators seventeenfold. But in the U.S., only 3 percent of waste is now disposed of in this way.

Incinerators are controversial in this country because of bad memories of older type incinerators whose odors were so pungent and objectionable; and because we feared that the fumes released in the burning waste were carcinogenic. We have also been concerned because the ash from incinerators must be treated as a hazardous waste. That is an appropriate concern. However, incineration does reduce total volume by between 70 percent and 90 percent, and is probably less dangerous to health than landfills, whose drawbacks are well documented.

There have been no national standards for incinerator emissions or dioxin levels. However, the new Clean Air Act will set those standards.

The federal government, aside from making RCRA actually work, could do two other things:

- Give as much air time and rhetoric to recycling as we currently give to drugs. Recycling requires fairly dramatic changes of mind. Concentrated public education has dramatically changed the way we view smoking and drunk driving in America. A concentrated public education program could just as dramatically change the way we look at recycling. Moreover, an aggressive national education program would also boost local efforts, which are too often isolated and for that reason seen by residents as ineffective.

- Create a clearinghouse for regional data on secondary markets, products, and processes that work. The secondary-use industry is in its infancy and a national informational network would not only stimulate recycling; it would lay the foundation for making better judgments about environmental costs of new materials production. Properly implemented, it could be a valuable industry resource.

Reuse and recycling, in short, far from being lightweight approaches to a heavyweight problem, are potentially among our most potent weapons in stemming world climate change. But they must be given priority—more priority than burning or burying.

Fixing It at the Tail Pipe

Eventually, emissions from motor vehicles must be eliminated.

As has so often been the case, California may be showing us the way we must go nationally. In December 1989, the California Air Resources Board announced a dramatic new program for further scaling back air-polluting emissions in that state.

As in Mexico City, the combination of people, cars, and geography has created a severe air-pollution problem in Southern California. Over thirteen million people live in the Los Angeles basin. Their numbers, their motor vehicles, and their total miles driven multiply daily. The periodic inversions—when the emis-

sions are trapped close to the ground—produce a hovering smog, which irritates the eyes, penetrates the lungs, and obscures the natural beauty of the basin.

The severity of the problem has generated an extraordinary response. Because California has been uniquely vulnerable to large-scale air pollution, it is the only state with authority under the federal Clean Air Act to impose restrictions more demanding than federal law. California has used that authority. It now requires emission controls on motor vehicles more demanding than on vehicles sold anywhere else in the world. Other states and the federal government are now considering adopting the "California Standards."

But even those standards, tough as they are, have been inadequate to deal with the enormous and growing problem in California. So, in December 1989, the California Air Resources Board announced a dramatic new and far-reaching proposal to further reduce motor vehicle emissions. The California proposals go far beyond anything now being considered under federal law. They would require expanded research and development on new fuels and engines to meet the new standards. In effect, they will require a new kind of automobile.

Although technical, the new standards would essentially require the development and sale in California of vehicles that would emit progressively smaller amounts of pollutants into the air. Labeled by the board as "transitional low-emission vehicles," "low-emission vehicles" (both using progressively cleaner fuels), and "ultra-low-emission vehicles" (powered entirely by electricity), these progressively cleaner cars would have to be sold in increasing numbers until the year 2003. By that time at least 15 percent of new vehicles sold in the state would have to be "ultra-low-emission vehicles"—electric cars. The rest would have to be "low-emission vehicles."

Electric-powered cars capable of performing on a par with gas-driven automobiles already exist. General Motors unveiled a prototype, the Impact, at the Los Angeles Auto Show in January

1990. The prototype tests quicker than 95 percent of the cars on the road today and is 100 percent less polluting. It accelerates from zero to sixty miles per hour in eight seconds, faster than both the Mazda Miata and the Nissan 3000ZX. Its need to re-charge its batteries every 125 miles is both a plus and a minus. The plus is that 125 miles is far enough to make it the first truly practical electric car. The minus is that 125 miles is still not far enough for longer commutes and cross-country travel. But the age of the electric car is dawning, and it could revolutionize the automobile's relationship to the environment. California is bank-ing on it.

To understand the magnitude of what California proposes to do, one need look no farther than its requirements on emissions of hydrocarbons. Hydrocarbons and nitrogen oxides emitted from motor vehicles are transformed into ozone when exposed to sunlight. Ozone is the principal ingredient in smog. Under current federal law, new cars must be certified to emit no more than 0.41 grams per mile (gpm) of hydrocarbons. California law will reduce that to 0.25 gpm, 0.075 gpm and, finally, with the ultra-low-emission vehicles, 0.04 gpm. Thus, in a little more than a decade, California will force a 90 percent reduction in hydro-carbon emissions.

At the same time, the board will require fuel suppliers to bring a much cleaner gasoline to power motor vehicles sold in Cali-fornia.

In a progress report issued in December 1989, the staff of the California Air Resources Board laid out the basis for the proposed program. Although the language of the report is spare and tech-nical, it captures the essence of the need for action: to reduce eye- and lung-irritating smog, to reduce the emissions that cause cancer, and to prevent further global warming. The report said in part:

> The overall objective of the proposal is to improve air quality in California. Gasoline-powered motor vehicles generate a sub-

stantial fraction of the emissions of ozone precursors, toxic air contaminants, and global warming gases in the state. The specific objective of this strategy is to reduce emissions of ozone precursors (reactive hydrocarbons and NO_x), CO, and toxic pollutants as much as possible, with a combination of advanced vehicle emission control technology and clean fuels.

1. Attaining ambient ozone and carbon monoxide standards will require more reductions of on-road vehicular emissions.

The board has adopted the *Post-1987 Motor Vehicle Plan,* which includes the recently adopted 0.25 gram/mile non-methane hydrocarbon standard, and it has approved an ambitious ozone attainment plan by the South Coast Air Quality Management District (SCAQMD). Even with the implementation of all measures known to be feasible, the air quality standards for ozone will be extremely difficult to meet. This proposal for low-emission vehicles and clean fuels would result in significantly lower emissions of hydrocarbons, CO, and NO_x.

2. Toxic pollutant emissions from motor vehicles pose a potential cancer risk.

Numerous toxic air contaminants, and potentially toxic air contaminants, have been identified in vehicular exhaust and evaporative emissions. At current emission rates, the potential incidence of cancer due to these vehicular emissions is estimated at 13,000 to 23,000 cases in the state over 70 years of continuous exposure. Many of these toxic pollutants, including benzene, formaldehyde, and 1,3-butadiene are generally reduced when exhaust hydrocarbon emissions are reduced. Benzene emissions can also be reduced by changing the composition of the fuel.

3. Motor vehicles are contributors to greenhouse gas emissions.

Motor vehicle exhaust emissions are a source of greenhouse gases (such as CO_2, methane, and nitrous oxide). The use of different fuels can result in different levels of greenhouse gas emissions. Evaluations to date show that there would likely be no adverse effect from a shift to cleaner fuels, and there could even be a net benefit. We will need to ensure that the proposed program has a favorable effect on global-warming emissions.

The result, if the proposals are adopted and implemented, will have significance beyond California, since about 15 per-

cent of all U.S. motor vehicles are sold in that state. In effect, California is setting standards for the entire U.S., and ultimately, the world. It is showing us the kind of tough-minded approach that will be necessary to slow and reverse global climate change.

14

What the Nations Must Do Together

National sovereignties with their boundaries and borders, even international conflicts with their conquests and their wars, will be irrelevant in the coming confrontation of the world's nations against global climate change. The nations must act and they must act together. These are some of the things they must do:

• They must, no matter how difficult it is or how long it takes, negotiate, sign, ratify, and implement an international accord for global protection. A Law of the Atmosphere treaty, proposed by the Canadians to limit the release of greenhouse gases and dangerous chemicals, and an Environmental Security Council, similar to the UN Security Council, are not too much to strive for.

As the United States moves aggressively to reduce air pollution, international agreements to require other countries to do likewise are essential to our competitiveness. Clean air is expensive. It is easier and cheaper for most industries to simply emit pollutants than to control or clean them up. People and the ecosystems pay the price.

If the developed nations, especially the United States, impose strict and expensive requirements on industries within their borders, less-developed nations that choose not to follow suit could become "pollution havens." Those nations could sacrifice the

health of their citizens for the immediate lure of jobs. A vigorous and unhealthy competition could develop in the search by industry for such pollution havens.

It is very much in the interest of a safe and healthy world as well as in the economic interest of the United States that such a situation not develop. Fair and balanced agreements which take into account the different economic and social circumstances of the participating nations could go a long way toward preventing such a development.

• They must find a satisfactory way to pay for the environmental war the nations must now wage together. A world atmosphere fund, financed by a tax on fossil fuel consumption, has been suggested. As I have said, responsible world bodies are working toward some kind of meaningful accord. It must include the wherewithal to bear the battle. We must do all we can as a nation to foster a meeting of minds worldwide, encourage it, participate in it, and help fund it.

• They must immediately convene a greenhouse summit of the world's nations to develop and implement a strategy. The U.S. should sponsor such a summit jointly with the Soviet Union. Gorbachev appears to be open to such a proposal. He has said that "we need an appropriate international policy in the field of ecology. Only if we formulate such a policy shall we be able to avert catastrophe. True, the elaboration of such a policy poses unconventional and difficult problems which sometimes affect the sovereignty of states. Yet it is a solvable problem."

On the agenda of such a greenhouse summit, at the very least, should be how to reduce carbon dioxide and other greenhouse gases, how to ban totally the use of CFCs, and how to reverse worldwide deforestation.

• They must call a Global Species Convention to shape an accord similar in spirit and scope to the other necessary international agreements. The appalling decimation of the earth's species must be stemmed.

• They must launch a major initiative, spearheaded by a pres-

tigious world panel, to develop a long-term strategy to fulfill national and world economic needs without destroying the global environment. This must take into account the basic truth that the options for rich, technologically advanced nations such as ours are numerous in the coming struggle, but for poorer nations they are few. It will be in the industrial world's interest to help the developing nations deal with environmental change. Gorbachev has suggested that it might be useful to institute a kind of international "Green Cross," patterned after the Red Cross, to lend assistance to states in ecological trouble. The idea is worth serious consideration.

• They must refine research and find better ways to more accurately monitor the planet's vital signs. We are now getting only vague impressions of the true rate of global warming and its impact on sea levels, agriculture, forests, water resources, and the cities. We have what the National Academy of Engineering's Robert M. White calls "an inverted pyramid: A huge and growing mass of proposals for policy action [to which I am adding mine] is balanced upon a handful of real facts. Data on likely causes are robust, though future emissions projections vary widely. Projections based upon mathematical approximations of atmospheric and oceanic conditions are credible but uncertain. Evidence from the climatic data is equivocal."

• They must, more than ever in the past, share their monitoring and research technologies, pool their reduction technologies, and devise mechanisms for sharing water in time of drought.

• They must devise an international code to govern those areas of technology that court high environmental risks. If we have learned anything over the past four decades it is that not all new technologies are benign. Some are deadly. At the heart of the matter is society's ever-rising dependence on rapidly devised, hurriedly deployed technologies whose complex side effects are unknown, unpredictable, or—most often—ignored. The ramifications of these technologies need to be known, predicted, and controlled. The last thing they need to be is ignored.

• They must find ways to promote programs leading to a stable world population of not more than nine billion people by the middle of the next century.

• They must launch a sustained international program to develop alternative fuels that do not generate carbon dioxide and the other greenhouse gases.

• They must reshape their foreign policies to spend less on military purchases and more on sustainable development.

• They must help create a strategy to forgive Third World countries their crushing debts if they will follow sustainable development practices in return. Or if that doesn't work, they must find some other way to help those nations undertake responsible development.

• They must reforest the earth—more than three hundred million acres of it that have been slashed and burned in the Third World countries. This effort is not moving fast enough. For every ten acres being cleared today in tropical regions, only one acre is being planted.

Attacking the Four Horsemen
Turning Down the Heat

A Greenhouse Emissions Control Protocol, similar to the Montreal Protocol for CFCs, is much needed, an appropriate first step in mounting our attack on the greenhouse gases. The generally conceded goal of scaling down CO_2 emissions by one-fifth by 2005 should be the minimum aspiration. I believe, with the Natural Resources Defense Council, that a variety of conservation and energy efficiency strategies could drop CO_2 emissions by 15 percent. I also believe, with the World Resources Institute, that policy choices made today and implemented over the next several decades could radically slow impending climate change and give us the precious time we need to deal with it. And I believe that the inverse side of that coin also holds: Unless policies are made

and implemented soon to limit greenhouse gas emissions, intolerable levels of global warming are a certainty.

The U.S. Environmental Protection Agency believes that CO_2 emissions would have to be slashed in half just to stabilize concentrations of greenhouse gases in the atmosphere. Methane would have to be cut by 10 to 20 percent, nitrous oxide by 40 percent, and CFCs virtually eliminated.

The EPA also believes there is no panacea, no single miracle cure-all that will get us to those reductions. It will require a battery of policy options. But when marshalled, such an array can have a dramatic effect. It might look like this:

- Automobiles averaging fifty miles per gallon of gas when new.
- Better still, automobiles powered by alternative fuels (e.g., solar-generated electricity) with zero emissions.
- Commercial buildings refitted to reduce their energy consumption by 40 percent.
- Single family homes requiring 90 percent less energy than they now do.
- A halt in global deforestation, replaced by a major reforestation program.
- A phaseout of CFCs.
- Emission fees on fossil fuels in proportion to their carbon content.
- A deep penetration of solar technologies into the energy market.
- A commitment of 5 percent of all newly planted forest and woodlands to biomass energy plantations.

This might do it. Of these, improvements in energy efficiency, reforestation, modernization of biomass use, and fees on carbon emissions look most promising in the short run—over the next few decades. Solar technologies and biomass plantations should

be pursued now. The measures that are most likely to reduce warming the most are those that change the fuel mix—whatever diminishes the use of fossil fuels and increases the available biomass. This could mean fees on fuels and wholesale planting of trees.

Saving the Ozone Layer

Since CFCs are not only ozone shredders, but potent greenhouse gases, limits must be clamped on their production and use and mandatory controls set on their escape into the atmosphere during manufacturing and disposal. The Montreal Protocol is now being renegotiated and rewritten to lock in a complete phaseout of CFCs by the turn of this century. During the phaseout, the U.S. should set the world an example by minimizing its CFC releases into the atmosphere. And during the phaseout the industrialized nations must make the technologies for alternatives available to developing countries on noncommercial terms. It is a goal well within our reach. Environmentally acceptable substitutes will be available by the early 1990s.

Stopping Acid Rain

To stop acid rain we must keep two chemicals out of the air —sulfur dioxide and nitrogen oxides. There are four known ways to do that. We can switch from high-sulfur to low-sulfur fuels. We can prevent the pollutants from forming during combustion. We can screen them, literally scrub them, from exhaust and flue gases. Or we can conserve energy and burn as little as possible of the fossil fuels that liberate these polluters into the atmosphere.

As with CFCs, the technology exists to eliminate most of the industrial emissions that produce the agents that cause acid rain. Available today are better energy efficiencies at the smokestack, although some of them are prohibitively expensive. New com-

bustion technologies are at hand. More effective pollution-control equipment has been developed. Fuel switching, although a potentially painful solution for miners in such economically strapped coal states as West Virginia, could be phased in. And to help offset the harm in the mines, the clean coal program should be vigorously pursued.

Wiser practices and better technologies are also available at the tail pipe. We can have stricter federal emission levels for cars, buses, and trucks and tighter inspection and maintenance procedures. It requires only the political will to act. We can use cleaner fuels, such as compressed natural gas and electricity, in commercial fleets and urban bus lines. We can install programs to cut the total number of vehicle miles travelled. We can improve traffic flow, develop better public transportation, reward car pools with preferred parking, and heighten the incentives for high-occupancy vehicles. We can certainly build cars that go farther on less fuel. Vehicles that get fifty miles per gallon are already on the road. Experiments suggest that cars capable of going eighty miles per gallon are possible with only modest advances over today's technology.

These are all options at the smokestack and the tail pipe, where the trouble begins. The major stumbling block has always been the cost of such programs: the cost of pollution control to utilities and the cost in unemployment to high-sulfur coal miners. We must find a way around those problems.

The situation cries out for an attack on all of acid rain's harmful pollutants across the board. Applying technology already available for desulfurizing flue gases and fuels, and using low-sulfur fuels to the greatest extent, SO_2 emissions in Europe could be halved in the next decade. In North America we can begin with the passage of adequate legislation in the U.S. Congress, and with a move toward a U.S.-Canada bilateral accord to cut sulfur dioxide emissions in half. The short-term goal should be to reduce the amount of sulfur dioxides seeping into the atmo-

sphere by ten million tons a year and nitrogen oxides by five million.

This is an attainable goal.

Rescuing the Rain Forest

A strong action plan to save what is left of the rain forests and replace some that have been lost is also already on the table. It was put together by an international task force convened by the World Resources Institute, the World Bank, and the United Nations Development Program. It calls for an $8 billion investment in the salvation of the world's narrow and tightening belt of tropical forests. The money would promote reforestation, protect water catchments and provide fuelwood, develop agroforestry systems, and define and manage national forest parks. A quarter of the money would go to make industrial use and management more efficient.

It is a credible plan. An international convention of nations to implement it is in order. The world's banking nations must work out an accommodation that meets the economic needs of the Third World countries where almost all of the rain forests lie and still conserves these precious cradles of life. We must push for an end to development assistance projects and programs that directly or indirectly inflict damage and deforestation. We must instead fund projects that further biodiversity and conservation. The nations of the world must begin to harvest only from areas where sustained yield management is practiced. And we must embrace economic policies that encourage new ideas for saving the endangered forests.

Epilogue

What would success look like? One writer has suggested that we will be able to say that we have made a serious commitment to solving the crisis if, by the end of this century, the nations have mandated fifty-mile-per-gallon auto fleets, set in motion a plan to phase out coal-fired power production, and installed aggressive energy efficiency and renewable energy development programs. He believes we will have made a serious commitment if worldwide spending on solar energy technologies has grown tenfold and if it is the energy source of choice for villages and suburbs worldwide by the end of this century.

I believe we will be able to say we are succeeding if we can look at the world and see our forest cover, particularly the rain forests, expanding instead of shrinking. I believe we will be able to say it if we can measure the volume of greenhouse gases in the atmosphere and see that if they are not decreasing, at least they are not increasing. I believe we will be able to say it if devastating droughts and floods are lessening, hunger is diminishing, and life expectancy is increasing. I believe we will be able to say it if the world we live in is a world of more simple transportation systems that no longer burn unconscionable volumes

of fossil fuels. I believe we will be able to say it if world population is beginning to stabilize, not because more people are dying, perhaps violently, but because fewer are being born. I believe we will be able to say it if the rain falling over our lakes and forests is acid-free. I believe we will be able to say we are succeeding when there is at last sunlight in Luisa's world and Eric is no longer afraid to go out into that sunlight.

Such a world might even be one where war has become irrelevant because the nations have united to fight an enemy much larger and more powerful than one another. Part of the requirement of waging and winning these environmental wars is to change the way we look at the world. A delegate to the Stockholm environmental meeting in 1972 said: "We live on only one earth but unfortunately we are not one people. But even the wretched of the earth want to belong to one earth." He then went on to ask pointedly, "Do the privileged want them in?" and then to say, "Ultimately, man will only succeed in removing or controlling the pollutants and other threats to the human environment when he has established on our small planet one people."

Men and women everywhere must unite against this the most serious threat to life in all of human history. If we are not united then we cannot succeed. United, we can survive.

We have done so much damage to our one earth in so short a time. David Brower, the noted environmentalist, put it in a most striking and graphic way in a lecture at the University of California in 1981:

> Compress the earth's time to the six-day creation, with Sunday midnight marking the beginning, and you find that life begins Tuesday noon, oil formation Saturday morning, dinosaurs on stage at four that afternoon and off stage by nine that evening, something like man five minutes before midnight but still Neanderthal eleven seconds before midnight. Not until one-and-a-half seconds before midnight did we take up agriculture, a quarter of a second Christianity, a fortieth of a second the Industrial Rev-

olution, and two-thousandth of a second the strange addiction to exponential growth in our attack on resources that are not renewable. It is midnight, and we find ourselves almost incorrigibly enchanted by the illusion that what worked so briefly can go on and on. It cannot.

Perhaps in the next two-thousandths of a second of the week to come we can redeem ourselves and the planet we've done so much to endanger.

If we do not succeed, if we do not rise to this occasion, if we do not rein in the four-decades-long chemical experiment we have been conducting on our one and only earth, we risk turning our world into a lifeless desert in the coming century, and bringing to pass the grim final environmental judgment of a world on fire. It is our obligation to see that this does not happen. Each of us is on this earth for a short time. We do not own forever the land we inherited from our ancestors. Rather we are stewards, holding the earth's natural resources in trust for our children and their children. We can and we must convey to them the very basics of healthy human life—clean air, pure water, unpoisoned land. The grim future that I pictured for the Erics and Luisas of the world, for all of our children, at the beginning of this book will happen—unless we act. I am committed to preventing it from happening. This country and this world must also be committed to it. Our lives depend upon it.

Sources

Acid Rain and Nonattainment Issues. Hearing before the Subcommittee on Environmental Protection of the Committee on Environment and Public Works, United States Senate, April 22, 1987.

Acid Rain Control Technologies. Hearings before the Subcommittee on Environmental Protection of the Committee on Environment and Public Works, United States Senate, March 4 and 11, 1987.

Angier, Natalie. "Bamboo Coaxed to Flower in Lab; Global Impact on the Crop Is Seen." *New York Times* (March 20, 1990).

Barth, Michael C., and James G. Titus. *Greenhouse Effect and Sea Level Rise: A Challenge for This Generation.* New York: Van Nostrand Reinhold, 1984.

Booth, William. "From Rain Forest to Grassland?" *Washington Post* (March 16, 1990).

———. "New Models Chill Some Predictions of Severely Overheated Earth." *Washington Post* (January 29, 1990).

Brodeur, Paul. "Annals of Chemistry: In the Face of Doubt." *The New Yorker* (June 9, 1986).

Brown, Lester R. "The Growing Grain Gap." *Worldwatch*, vol. 1, no. 5 (September-October, 1988).

Brown, Lester R., Christopher Flavin, and Sandra Postel. "No Time to Waste." *Worldwatch*, vol. 2, no. 1 (January-February, 1989).

227

Brown, Lester R., and John E. Young. "Growing Food in a Warmer World." *Worldwatch*, vol. 1, no. 6 (November-December, 1988).

Brown, Lester R., et al. *State of the World 1989*. New York: W. W. Norton, 1989.

Brown, Martha. "Tropical Rain Forests: Stronghold of Biological Diversity." *Western Wildlands* (Winter 1988).

Browne, Malcolm W. "In Protecting the Atmosphere, Choices Are Costly and Complex." *New York Times* (March 7, 1989).

Bureau of National Affairs. *World Climate Change Report*. Prototype Edition, vol. 1, nos. 1 (September 1989), 2 (October 1989), 3 (November 1989), 4 (December 1989).

Carson, Rachel. *Silent Spring*. Boston: Houghton Mifflin, 1962.

Clark, William C. "Managing Planet Earth." *Scientific American*, vol. 261, no. 3 (September 1989).

Clean Air Act Amendments of 1987. Hearings before the Subcommittee on Environmental Protection of the Committee on Environment and Public Works, United States Senate, Part 1, June 16–17, 1987.

Congressional Research Service. *Acid Rain: A Survey of Data and Current Analyses*. A report for the House Subcommittee on Health and the Environment of the Committee on Energy and Commerce (Washington, 1984).

————. *Agriculture, Forestry, and Global Climate Change—A Reader*. A report prepared for the Committee on Agriculture, Nutrition, and Forestry, United States Senate (April 1989).

————. *The Global Environment*. CRS Review (August 1989).

Crosson, Pierre R., and Norman J. Rosenberg. "Strategies for Agriculture." *Scientific American*, vol. 261, no. 3 (September 1989).

Durning, Alan. "Cradles of Life." *Worldwatch*, vol. 2, no. 3 (May-June 1989).

Ehrlich, Paul R., and Anne H. Ehrlich. *The Population Explosion*. New York: Simon & Schuster, 1990.

El-Hinnawi, Essam, and Manzur H. Hashmi. *The State of the Environment*. London: Butterworths, 1987.

Environmental Protection Agency. *The Potential Effects of Global Climate Change on the United States*. Draft report to Congress. 2 vols. and Executive Summary (Washington 1988).

————. *Policy Options for Stabilizing Global Climate*. Draft report to Congress. 2 vols. and Executive Summary (Washington 1989).

Farman, Joseph, et al. "Large Losses of Total Ozone in Antarctica Reveal Seasonal ClO$_x$/NO$_x$ Interaction." *Nature* (May 16, 1985).

Fisher, Arthur. "One Model to Fit All." *Mosaic*, vol. 19, no. 3/4 (Fall/Winter 1988).

Flavin, Christopher. "The Case Against Reviving Nuclear Power." *Worldwatch*, vol. 1, no. 4 (July-August 1988).

———. "The Heat Is On." *Worldwatch*, vol. 1, no. 6 (November-December 1988).

French, Hilary F. "An Environmental Security Council?" *Worldwatch*, vol. 2, no. 5 (September-October 1989).

———. "The Greening of the Soviet Union." *Worldwatch*, vol. 2, no. 3 (May-June 1989).

———. "Restoring the U.N." *Worldwatch*, vol. 1, no. 4 (July-August 1988).

Gibbons, John H., Peter D. Blair, and Holly L. Gwin. "Strategies for Energy Use." *Scientific American*, vol. 261, no. 3 (September 1989).

The Global Environmental Protection Act of 1988. Joint hearings before the Subcommittee on Hazardous Wastes and Toxic Substances and the Subcommittee on Environmental Protection of the Committee on Environment and Public Works, United States Senate, September 14 and 16, 1988.

Global Warming and Its Implications for California. Hearing before the Committee on Energy and Natural Resources, United States Senate, Santa Monica, CA, May 20, 1989.

Gorbachev, Mikhail. Address to the Global Forum of Spiritual and Parliamentary Leaders on Human Survival. Moscow, January 19, 1990.

Graedel, Thomas E., and Paul J. Crutzen. "The Changing Atmosphere." *Scientific American*, vol. 261, no. 3 (September 1989).

Gushee, David E. *Global Climate Change and the Greenhouse Effect: Congressional Activity and Options.* CRS Issue Brief (November 2, 1988).

———. *Stratospheric Ozone Depletion: Regulatory Issues.* CRS Issue Brief (October 17, 1989).

Health Effects of Acid Rain Precursors. Hearing before the Subcommittee on Environmental Protection of the Committee on Environment and Public Works, United States Senate, February 3, 1987.

Health Effects of Air Pollution. Hearing before the Subcommittee on Environmental Protection of the Committee on Environment and Public Works, United States Senate, April 18, 1989.

Heise, Lori. "Air Pollution Attacks China's Forests." *Worldwatch*, no. 1, vol. 1 (January-February 1988).

Jacobsen, Judith. *Promoting Population Stabilization: Incentives for Small Families.* Worldwatch Paper 54 (June 1983).

Jacobson, Jodi L. *Environmental Refugees: A Yardstick of Habitability.* Worldwatch Paper 86 (November 1988).

———. "Recent Floods are 'Unnatural Disasters'." *Worldwatch*, vol. 1, no. 6 (November-December 1989).

———. "Swept Away." *Worldwatch*, vol. 2, no. 1 (January-February 1989).

Keyfitz, Nathan. "The Growing Human Population." *Scientific American*, vol. 261, no. 3 (September 1989).

Lemonick, Michael D. "Antarctica: Is Any Place Safe from Mankind?" *Time*, vol. 135, no. 3 (January 15, 1990).

Lenssen, Nick. "Debt for Nature Swaps." *Worldwatch*, vol. 1, no. 6 (November-December 1989).

Lowe, Marcia D. "The Sahara Swallows Mauritania." *Worldwatch*, vol. 1, no. 5 (September-October 1988).

Machado, Sheila, and Rick Piltz. *Reducing the Rate of Global Warming: The States' Role.* Renew America (November 1988).

MacKenzie, James J. *Breathing Easier: Taking Action on Climate Change, Air Pollution, and Energy Insecurity.* World Resources Institute (July 1989).

MacKenzie, James J., and Mohamed T. El-Ashry. *Ill Winds: Airborne Pollution's Toll on Trees and Crops.* World Resources Institute (September 1988).

McNamara, Robert S. "Time Bomb or Myth: The Population Problem." *Foreign Affairs*, vol. 62, no. 5 (Summer 1984).

MacNeill, Jim. "Strategies for Sustainable Economic Development." *Scientific American*, vol. 261, no. 3 (September 1989).

Manson, Alex N. "Acid Rain: The Canadian Perspective." *State Government News*, September 1988.

Mathews, Jessica T. "Global Climate Change: Toward a Greenhouse Policy." *Issues in Science and Technology*, Spring 1987.

Maurits la Riviere, J. W. "Threats to the World's Water." *Scientific American*, vol. 261, no. 3 (September 1989).

Miller, Alan S., and Irving M. Mintzer. *The Sky Is the Limit: Strategies for Protecting the Ozone Layer*. World Resources Institute (November 1986).

Mintzer, Irving M. *A Matter of Degrees: The Potential for Controlling the Greenhouse Effect*, World Resources Institute (April 1987).

Mitchell, George J. "Statement of Senator George J. Mitchell." College of the Atlantic, Bar Harbor, ME, August 14, 1988.

————. "Saving the Environment." Address, Canadian Club, Toronto, Canada, June 28, 1989.

Molina, Mario, and F. Sherwood Rowland. "Stratospheric Sink for Chlorofluoromethanes: Chlorine Atom Catalyzed Destruction of Ozone." *Nature* (June 28, 1974).

Morrison, Robert E. *Global Climate Change*. CRS Issue Brief (October 6, 1989).

Myers, Norman. "The Heat Is On: Global Warming Threatens the Natural World." *Greenpeace*, vol. 14, no. 3 (May/June, 1989).

————. *Not Far Afield: U.S. Intersts and the Global Environment*. World Resources Institute (June 1987).

National Academy of Sciences, National Academy of Engineering, and Institute of Medicine. *Global Environmental Change: Recommendations for President Elect George Bush*. Washington, 1988.

National Energy Policy Act of 1988 and Global Warming. Hearings before the Committee on Energy and Natural Resources, United States Senate, August 11, September 19 and 20, 1988.

National Global Change Research Act of 1989. Hearing before the Committee on Commerce, Science, and Transportation, United States Senate, February 22, 1989.

Nelson, Mark M. "Darkness at Noon: As Shroud of Secrecy Lifts in Europe, Smog Shroud Emerges." *Wall Street Journal* (March 1, 1990).

Oppenheimer, Michael, and Robert H. Boyle. *Dead Heat: The Race Against the Greenhouse Effect*. New York: Basic Books, 1990.

Ozone Depletion, the Greenhouse Effect and Climate Change. Joint hearing before the Subcommittees on Environmental Protection and Hazardous Wastes and Toxic Substances of the Committee on Environment and Public Works, United States Senate, Part 2, January 28, 1987.

Postel, Sandra. "A Green Fix to the Global Warm-Up." *Worldwatch*, vol. 1, no. 5 (September-October 1988).

———. *Air Pollution, Acid Rain, and the Future of Forests*, Worldwatch Paper 58 (March 1984).

———. *Altering the Earth's Chemistry: Assessing the Risks*. Worldwatch Paper 71 (July 1986).

———. "Land's End." *Worldwatch*, vol. 2 no. 3 (May-June 1989).

Postel, Sandra, and Lori Heise. *Reforesting the Earth*. Worldwatch Paper 83 (April 1988).

The Potential Impact of Global Warming on Agriculture. Hearing before the Committee on Agriculture, Nutrition, and Forestry, United States Senate, December 1, 1988.

Reid, Walter V., and Kenton R. Miller. *Keeping Options Alive: The Scientific Basis for Conserving Biodiversity*, World Resources Institute (October 1989).

Renner, Michael G. "Forging Environmental Alliances." *Worldwatch*, vol. 2, no. 6 (November-December 1989).

———. "Guns Over Butter." *Worldwatch*, vol. 1, no. 4 (July-August 1988).

Repetto, Robert. "Population, Resources, Environment: An Uncertain Future." *Population Bulletin*, vol. 42, no. 2 (April 1989 Reprint).

Repetto, Robert, ed. *The Global Possible: Resources, Development, and the New Century*. New Haven, CT: Yale University Press, 1985.

Roan, Sharon. *Ozone Crisis: The 15-Year Evolution of a Sudden Global Emergency*. New York: Wiley, 1989.

Ruckelshaus, William D. "Toward a Sustainable World." *Scientific American*, vol. 261, no. 3 (September 1989).

Schneider, Stephen H. "The Changing Climate." *Scientific American*, vol. 261, no. 3 (September 1989).

———. *Global Warming: Are We Entering the Greenhouse Century?* San Francisco: Sierra Club Books, 1989.

Shea, Cynthia Pollock. "Holes Emerge in Ozone Treaty." *Worldwatch*, vol. 1, no. 6 (November-December 1988).

———. *Protecting Life on Earth: Steps to Save the Ozone Layer*. Worldwatch Paper 87 (December 1988).

Simons, Marlise. "Vast Amazon Fires, Man-Made, Linked to Global Warming." *New York Times* (August 12, 1988).

Stolarski, Richard S. "The Antarctic Ozone Hole." *Scientific American*, vol. 258, no. 1 (January 1988).

Stratospheric Ozone Depletion. Joint hearing before the Subcommittees on Hazardous Wastes and Toxic Substances and Environmental Protection of the Committee on Environment and Public Works, United States Senate, March 30, 1988.

Stratospheric Ozone Depletion and Chlorofluorocarbons. Joint hearings before the Subcommittees on Environmental Protection and Hazardous Wastes and Toxic Substances of the Committee on Environment and Public Works, United States Senate, May 12, 13, and 14, 1987.

Tiemann, Mary, and Susan R. Fletcher. *International Environment: Overview of Major Issues*. Congressional Research Service Issue Brief (October 13, 1989).

Tolba, Mostafa Kamal, ed. *Evolving Environmental Perceptions: From Stockholm to Nairobi*. London: Butterworths, 1988.

"Torching the Amazon: Can the Rain Forest Be Saved?" *Time*, vol. 134, no. 12 (September 18, 1989).

Train, Russell E. Fundraising letter, World Wildlife Fund (1989).

Udall, James R. "Turning Down the Heat." *Sierra*, vol. 74, no. 4 (July-August 1989).

"Update: The Oceans & Global Warming." *Oceanus*, vol. 32, no. 2 (Summer 1989).

"The Vanishing Jungle." *The Economist*, October 15, 1988.

White, Robert M. "Greenhouse Policy and Climate Uncertainty." *Bulletin American Meterological Society*, vol. 70, no. 9 (September 1989).

Wilson, Edward O. "Threats to Biodiversity." *Scientific American*. vol. 261, no. 3 (September 1989).

Wolf, Edward C. *On the Brink of Extinction: Conserving the Diversity of Life*. Worldwatch Paper 78 (June 1987).

World Commission on Environment and Development. *Our Common Future*. (Oxford: Oxford University Press, 1987).

World Resources Institute. *Changing Climate: A Guide to the Greenhouse Effect* (January 1989).

———. *The Crucial Decade: The 1990s and the Global Environmental Challenge* (January 1989).

———. *Keep Tropical Forests Alive* (September 1986).

World Resources Institute and National Climate Program Office National Oceanic and Atmospheric Administration. *Strategic Planning Seminar on the Long-Term Implications of Climatic Change* (January 5, 1988).

World Resources Institute, the World Bank, and the United Nations Development Programme. *Tropical Forests: A Call for Action* (October 1985).

Young, John E. "Acid Rain, Acid Waters." *Worldwatch*, vol. 1, no. 5 (September-October 1988).

Zurer, Pamela. "Nations Urged to Unite in Efforts to Stem Global Climate Change." *Chemical & Engineering News*, May 15, 1989.

Index

About the Author

George J. Mitchell has served as Senate Majority Leader since 1988. Appointed to the Senate in 1980 to fill the seat of Edmund Muskie, he was reelected in 1982 and in 1988.

Before his appointment to the Senate, Senator Mitchell served as Assistant County Attorney for Cumberland County, U.S. Attorney for Maine, and as a U.S. District Court judge. With Senator William S. Cohen of Maine, he is coauthor of *Men of Zeal*, which describes the investigation of the Iran-Contra affair by the Senate Iran-Contra panel, of which he was a member. Mitchell has one daughter, Andrea, and resides in Portland, Maine.